THE LAYMAN'S GUIDE TO
SCOTLAND'S LAW

Important Note

The questions and answers in this book reflect the law as it stands at 1 February 1995.

The Layman's Guide To Scotland's Law

CAMERON FYFE

MAINSTREAM
PUBLISHING

EDINBURGH AND LONDON

First published in Great Britain in 1995 by
MAINSTREAM PUBLISHING COMPANY (EDINBURGH) LTD
7 Albany Street
Edinburgh EH1 3UG

ISBN 1 85158 718 7

A catalogue record for this book is available from
the British Library

The author has donated all royalties from this book to the
Leukaemia Research Fund

Typeset in Garamond by Pioneer Associates Ltd., Perthshire
Printed in Great Britain by HarperCollins Manufacturing, Glasgow

Contents

Introduction

Open most law books and what do you find? Legalese, words you have never seen before and, worst of all, Latin phrases, all tied together with complicated phrases only lawyers understand. This book is an attempt to demystify the law and to offer a brief guide to one or two topics by way of straightforward questions and answers.

The choice of topics is not haphazard. Over the last few years my firm has operated a 24-hour free advice line which people ring most of the day and a good part of the night. We have received literally thousands of calls from the public seeking legal advice. I carried out a survey to find out which aspects of the law attracted the most questions and it is these topics which appear in this book. *The Layman's Guide to Scotland's Law* should therefore offer a useful and comprehensive guide to the most common legal problems.

I have always found that most clients who ask me

for advice are looking for a concise answer to their question. They certainly do not want a long, rambling dissertation which leaves them more confused and uncertain than before. If, for instance, a client asks if he can write a will leaving his entire estate to his girl-friend rather than his wife, he wants a simple yes or no. He does not want to know what some Judge in the eighteenth century had to say about it all. This book attempts to give short, snappy answers to such questions.

Inevitably, one or two subjects overlap (for instance, divorce and the Child Support Agency) and a couple of questions therefore appear under more than one topic. I hope this will save readers having to jump from one topic to another in their quest for an answer.

Any reader who seeks any further advice on the topics raised in this book (or indeed any other legal topic) should use our Freefone number which is 0800 11 12 13.

I would like to thank the staff and fellow Partners at Ross Harper & Murphy for all their help. In particular I owe thanks to my Partner Robert Brown, my office manager Karen Cettiga, and my secretary Tracey Shanley. I would also like to thank my clients who kindly gave permission to print the various anecdotes in the book which I have used to throw light on the points of law in question.

The Law and Your Family

Marriage

The legal formalities of a marriage ceremony are fairly straightforward. For instance, a client of mine (for whom I later obtained an annulment) got married during his coffee break.

You are legally married once both parties say the magic words 'I do'. There is a reported case of a man who was in the process of summoning up the courage to say 'I do' when he lost his nerve and shouted out to those congregated in the church, 'Oh, God – I can't go through with this!' He then ran full speed down the aisle and out of the church and apparently kept running until he was in the next postal district. The court decided that there was no marriage because he had not said 'I do'.

There is no limit to the time you require to be married before you can proceed with a divorce action. I knew of a case in which the marriage broke down at the wedding reception. The bride's father started to make derogatory remarks about his new son-in-law in his speech. The incensed bridegroom let fly with a left hook which brought the speech to a premature end. There was then a bit of a rabble during which the bridegroom assaulted his new wife and started to rant and rave at her in front of all the guests. She considered that the marriage had broken down and began divorce proceedings.

Q. At what age can I legally get married?

A. Sixteen.

Q. Do I require to give notice to anyone that I am getting married?

A. A Notice of Intention to Marry must be submitted by you and your partner to the Registrar in the district in which the marriage is to take place. You both also require to submit your Birth Certificates, Extract Marriage Certificate and Divorce Decree in relation to any previous marriage and, if you are a widow or widower, the Death Certificate of your former spouse.

Q. Do I have to have a witness at the marriage ceremony?

A. You must arrange for two witnesses to be present at the marriage ceremony. They require to be at least 16 years of age.

Q. Does being married alter my tax status?

A. There is a tax benefit in being married in that there is an addition to your personal allowance, known as Married Couples Allowance. (Husbands and wives are treated as two separate people for most taxation purposes.)

Q. What is the position if I discover my wife is already married to someone else?

A. If your wife was married to someone else at the time of your marriage, then your marriage is invalid and has no legal effect. Furthermore your wife may be charged with the crime of bigamy (which is the crime of entering into a marriage when you know that you are already married to someone else). You would be advised to have the marriage wiped off the record books by raising an action for annulment of marriage in the Court of Session in Edinburgh.

Q. Is it against the law for me to marry my cousin or any other relative?

A. You are entitled to marry your cousin. It is against the law to marry certain other relatives including your brother, sister, grandparent, grandchild, aunt, uncle, stepmother or stepfather.

Q. What is a prenuptial agreement and would such a document stand up in court?

A. A prenuptial agreement is one entered into with your partner, prior to your marriage. One partner might agree for instance to make no claim on the other's capital in the event of a separation. Such an agreement does stand and is legally enforceable. However, either partner can apply to the court to have the agreement set aside if he or she can prove that it is unfair and unreasonable.

Q. My partner and I are living together but are not married. He would like to adopt my child. Can we do so?

A. Adoption is not possible unless you are married. Furthermore, the child's father requires to consent to the adoption (although that consent can be dispensed with if it is being unreasonably withheld – *see* ACCESS AND CUSTODY OF CHILDREN, page 61).

Q. If I get married in a foreign country, is that marriage valid in Scotland?

A. Yes, provided the marriage is carried out in accordance with the formalities required for marriage in that particular country.

Q. At what point in the ceremony does the marriage actually become valid?

A. The marriage becomes valid once both parties have said the words 'I do'.

Divorce

First Steps After Your Marriage Breaks Up

It is often the case that those legal steps which you take just after your marriage has broken up are the ones which turn out to be the most important. If, for instance, you are contemplating a claim for capital against your husband, he may be tempted to dispose of his capital. I acted for one husband who transferred all his stocks and shares to his son's name. Another withdrew all the money from his building society account and put it on a horse (which lost). In each case the wife would have been well advised to obtain a court order against her husband to prevent him disposing of his assets in this way.

Precautionary steps should also be taken where there is a joint bank account. I acted for one woman who had a joint account containing around £8,000, and whose husband left her for another woman.

Presumably in an attempt to impress his new partner, he withdrew the entire £8,000 and took her on an extravagant cruise which, legally, he was entitled to do. When my client came to see me for advice, it was too late. By that time her husband was halfway across the Mediterranean. My advice to her would have been to withdraw £4,000 from the account or to have asked the bank to freeze the entire account.

If you seek maintenance for your children you now require to apply to the Child Support Agency (unless the sum you are seeking is very high, in which case you can ask the court for an order for maintenance). Unfortunately, however, the Child Support Agency is not particularly quick in obtaining the maintenance. Some of my clients have had to wait for several months. Until the Child Support Agency is reorganised, there would appear to be no way round this.

In this chapter the words 'husband' and 'wife' are interchangeable.

Q. What should be my first step when my marriage breaks up?

A. Go and see your lawyer immediately. There is much advice he or she can give you to protect your position and inform you of your rights.

Q. What should I do if there is money in our joint bank account?

A. You should consider withdrawing half of the funds just in case your spouse decides to withdraw the entire contents of the account. Alternatively, you could ask the bank to freeze the account to prevent your spouse withdrawing any money from it. The bank should do this upon your request. There is no need to have a lawyer's letter, for example.

Q. If I wish to make a claim against my husband's capital can I do anything to stop him from disposing of that capital?

A. Yes. You can obtain a court order called an interim interdict against your husband if you are reasonably apprehensive that he will act in this way. You can also freeze any money in his bank account or building society account if you believe that he may try to dispose of these funds.

Q. Can my spouse put me out of the matrimonial home?

A. No. You have every right to remain in the house even if it is in your spouse's name. (Your spouse may, however, obtain a court order to evict you if you are violent or if your behaviour is intolerable and is affecting your spouse's health.)

Q. Can I put my spouse out of the house?

A. Similarly, you can only do this if your spouse is violent or is behaving intolerably to the detriment of your health. This is the case even if the house is in your spouse's name.

Q. What can I do if my spouse locks me out of the house?

A. You should inform the police who may assist you in re-entering the house. Failing that, you can apply to the court for an order to enter the house. This is called an order for occupancy rights.

Q. How quickly can I obtain maintenance for my children?

A. You should immediately contact the Child Support Agency who will thereafter intimate a claim to your spouse. Your spouse is liable to make payment from the date of the intimation. However, there are presently substantial delays on the part of the Child Support Agency.

Q. How quickly can I obtain maintenance for myself?

A. You can apply to the court for an award of maintenance within a matter of a few weeks. (If, however, you are eligible for legal aid you would have to await the outcome of your legal aid application.)

Q. Do I have to allow my spouse access to my children?

A. In theory yes, on the basis that you both have joint custody in the absence of any court order. In practice, however, your spouse cannot enforce access without obtaining a court order (although he could snatch the child – *see below*). It is usually in your children's interests to allow your spouse access as quickly as possible.

Q. What should I do if I am worried that my spouse may try to remove the children from my care?

A. You can obtain an interim interdict against your spouse from removing the children. Any breach of the interim interdict by your spouse would be regarded very seriously by the court and may even be an imprisonable offence.

Q. If I leave the matrimonial home, is there anything I should do in respect of electricity accounts, etc?

A. You should write to the authorities involved (British Telecom, etc) and advise them to take the account out of your name or out of the joint names of you and your spouse. From that date, you are no longer liable for these accounts.

Grounds for Divorce

There are five grounds for divorce, the most common being adultery, desertion and unreasonable behaviour. Virtually any behaviour can be defined as 'unreasonable' if a person's health has suffered as a result of it. I knew of a man whose wife became infatuated with a BBC newsreader. Not only was her bedroom wall plastered with magazine and newspaper cuttings of her idol, but she often taped his voice from the TV or radio and played it back time and again at an uncomfortably loud volume. Her husband eventually had to consult his doctor as her behaviour was having such an adverse affect on his health. This was sufficient to obtain a divorce.

Sometimes the behaviour complained of by the client can be stranger than fiction. I knew of a case in which a young married couple shared a small house in one of Glasgow's large housing estates. To make some extra money they took in a female lodger who slept on the couch. The husband could not contain his lustful desire for the lodger and began sneaking downstairs in the small hours to join her on the couch, while his wife turned a blind eye. Finding the couch uncomfortable and restrictive, he then insisted that the lodger be allowed to share the double bed with his wife. Again, the wife accepted this. After a few weeks he told his wife that she should sleep on the couch to allow him and the lodger the privacy of the double bed. Unbelievably, his wife obeyed the order and indeed put up with the situation for a couple of months before contacting a lawyer to ask if her husband's behaviour was unreasonable enough to merit a divorce.

People's perception of what constitutes unreasonable behaviour can therefore differ widely. At one extreme I've had clients complain about behaviour which to the vast majority of the population would seem entirely reasonable. These have included playing golf on a Sunday, choice of television programmes and taste in ties. It sometimes occurred to me that criticism of such behaviour was in itself probably grounds for divorce. It reminded me of Woody Allen's line about his first wife: 'The problem was that she was very immature. For instance, she would often come into the bathroom when I was having a bath and would deliberately sink all my boats.'

Verbal abuse has long been recognised by the courts as a constituent of unreasonable behaviour. I remember once asking a client if her violent and drunken husband had also been verbally abusive to her. 'No,' she replied. 'He often calls me a cow but nothing abusive.' One of my worst moments was with a client who was particularly reticent about telling me details of the breakdown of the marriage (which is understandable). Obtaining the required information was like pulling teeth. I asked her if her husband had been verbally abusive towards her. She replied that he had. I asked her if she could give me a couple of examples. She replied that she was too embarrassed to tell me. To try and help her I said, 'Did he ever call you a cow or a whore?' 'He certainly did not!' she replied as she stormed out of the office. I was very young at the time.

Q. Can I raise an action of divorce immediately?

A. Yes, if you raise the divorce on the grounds of your partner's unreasonable behaviour or adultery.

Q. What constitutes unreasonable behaviour?

A. Basically any behaviour which causes your health to suffer. You must have a witness who can confirm most of the details of your spouse's alleged behaviour.

Q. What do I have to prove in order to obtain a divorce on the grounds of adultery?

A. You have to prove that your partner is probably having an affair. Evidence that your partner is living with or has gone on holiday with the lover is normally sufficient.

Q. Can I raise a divorce action even though I am still living with my partner?

A. Yes, provided there is little communication between you and you have ceased to have sexual relations.

Q. How can I obtain a divorce if I do not have grounds for unreasonable behaviour or adultery?

A. You can raise a divorce once you have been separated from your partner for two years (provided your partner is prepared to consent to the divorce).

Q. Can my partner give consent and then withdraw it?

A. Yes, right up to the last minute.

Q. What can I do if my partner refuses to agree to a divorce?

A. You can raise a divorce action, without your partner's consent, once you have been apart for five years. You can also divorce on the grounds of desertion.

Q. What is desertion?

A. You can divorce your partner on these grounds if you can show:
(1) you have been apart for two years;
(2) at the time your partner left you were prepared to carry on married life;
(3) you gave your partner no reasonable cause for leaving you;
(4) you have not refused any reasonable offer to go back to your partner.

Q. What is a 'simplified action' for divorce?

A. This is a very quick and cheap form of obtaining a divorce. It can be raised after five years (or two years if your partner consents) provided there are no children of the marriage and there is no financial dispute.

Q. When deciding the financial aspects of a divorce, does the court take into account whose fault it was that the marriage broke down?

A. No. The question of fault is generally irrelevant to all financial considerations.

Adultery

Adultery can be very difficult to prove. It must be frustrating for a woman who sees her husband entering a cinema with his lover only to be told that this evidence is not sufficient. It is particularly difficult to prove when the unfaithful partner to the marriage (usually the husband, I have to say) is aware that his wife is attempting to obtain evidence of the adultery. I recall a case in which the husband deliberately took steps to mislead his wife and put her on the wrong trail. He manufactured a letter which he left lying around their home which indicated that he and his lover intended to spend the next weekend in the Lake District. At considerable expense to the client we arranged for private investigators to set up camp outside the hotel in Grasmere only to discover later that her husband had spent an amorous weekend in Speyside with his mistress.

I heard of another case in which the client advised her solicitor that she suspected her husband of having an affair. Among other things she had noticed make-up on his shirt collar. The solicitor instructed private investigators to follow the husband around and to report on their findings. When the investigators finalised the report they sent it back to the lawyer with a note attached suggesting that he might want to break the news gently to the client – their report concluded that the husband was having an affair with his wife's mother. Even the most cynical solicitor is rarely unmoved by the heartbreak that adultery can bring about.

In another case a solicitor was instructed by a man who was convinced that his wife was committing adultery. The solicitor instructed a private investigator whom he had used for several years and had always found to be quick and efficient. In this particular case, however, the investigator failed to produce his report in the usual two to three-week period. Once three months had gone by and after several gentle reminders, the solicitor phoned the investigator to ask if there was a problem. The investigator sheepishly confessed that he in fact was the man who was having the affair with the client's wife. Another firm of investigators were then instructed and the divorce was obtained within three months.

Q. What do I have to prove in order to divorce my spouse on the grounds of adultery?

A. You require to prove that your spouse is *probably* having sexual intercourse with someone else.

Q. Would evidence of holding hands in the pub or being seen together at the cinema be sufficient?

A. No. Evidence of a sexual relationship would require to be stronger than that. For instance, if one went to the other's flat and was still there in the small hours, that would probably be enough.

Q. Is evidence that they have been on holiday together sufficient?

A. Usually, yes.

Q. If I cannot prove adultery but can show that my spouse is out most nights socialising with the opposite sex, is this enough?

A. No, but this may allow you to divorce your spouse on the grounds of unreasonable behaviour (*see* GROUNDS FOR DIVORCE, page 22).

Q. How many witnesses are required to confirm the affair?

A. Two witnesses. They can be friends or relatives or, failing that, private investigators who might follow your spouse to obtain the required evidence.

Q. So it is not necessary to hire a private investigator?

A. No. You and a friend or relative could follow your spouse around or wait outside his flat to obtain the required evidence. Many private investigators are highly trained in this type of work, however.

Q. If I did hire a private investigator, what information would be required?

A. He would need a photograph of you and of your spouse as well as any information you have which has led you to suspect that your spouse is having an affair. The photographs are required so that the investigator can identify your spouse and can confirm to the court that your spouse's lover is not you.

Q. If adultery takes place after my spouse and I have separated, is that still grounds for divorce?

A. Yes. It does not matter how long after the date of separation the adultery takes place.

Q. If I forgive my spouse's adultery, can I later raise a divorce action on the basis of that adultery?

A. No, if six months have gone by from the date of the adultery.

Q. **If my husband and I both want a divorce and it is therefore arranged for him to have an affair with someone else, is that still grounds for divorce?**

A. No. This would be regarded as a 'set-up' by the court and would not be acceptable.

Q. **If I cannot prove adultery, what are the other grounds for divorce?**

A. There are four other grounds:
  (1) unreasonable behaviour;
  (2) desertion (if you have been apart for two years and you gave your spouse no reasonable cause for leaving);
  (3) two years' separation (if your spouse consents);
  (4) five years' separation (whether your spouse consents or not).

Q. **If I raise a divorce action against my spouse and then I commit adultery, am I still entitled to go ahead with my divorce?**

A. Yes.

Q. **Who pays for a divorce on the grounds of adultery?**

A. If you win the divorce, then your spouse requires to pay. Your spouse's lover cannot be liable.

Q. Would the court take the adultery into account when deciding financial claims upon divorce?

A. No, the court generally does not take into account whose fault it was that the marriage broke down when deciding financial matters.

Financial Claims upon Divorce

There are several steps you can take to safeguard your position if you anticipate that your marriage might break up. Many women come to us seeking to claim a capital payment from their husbands, but they sometimes have little information or documentation regarding their husband's financial position. I knew of one wise woman who pretended to her husband that their marriage was all sweetness and light while she photocopied every financial document he kept in his chest of drawers. Furthermore, on the day she left him, she withdrew all the money from their three joint bank accounts and removed all items of furniture from their home (although she left him the kettle so he could make himself a cup of tea). As a result, when it came to negotiating a capital claim, she held a hand full of aces.

Some divorces are reasonably amicable. Others, especially where there are financial claims, are not. The husband of one client agreed to give his wife the family piano but not the piano stool. I heard of a case in which a woman had found out that her husband was having an affair with his secretary. She left the matrimonial home in disgust and raised a divorce action against her husband, seeking fairly substantial sums of money. He was willing to agree to virtually anything for a life of peace with his newfound love. Virtually the day after a matrimonial agreement had been drawn up and signed, he returned home to discover an unpleasant smell in the living-room. As each day went by the smell became worse and was soon unbearable. It was well over a week before he discovered that his wife had sewn prawns and shrimps into his curtains. At least she had the sense to wait until the agreement had been signed.

Q. Am I entitled to claim maintenance from my husband for my children?

A. Yes, provided your husband's income is sufficient to merit such a claim. If he is working or is receiving a reasonably high amount of benefit, he will normally be liable for maintenance. Your claim must be made through the Child Support Agency (unless the amount you are seeking is very high). The court is still entitled to increase or reduce existing awards of aliment up to April 1996. (If you are receiving Income Support, however, the Agency presently arranges any increase or reduction in the aliment.)

Q. Am I entitled to claim maintenance for myself?

A. Yes. You will normally be entitled to this maintenance (called periodical allowance) if you are unemployed and your husband is working, or if you are both working but his salary is substantially higher than yours.

Q. For how long is he liable to pay me periodical allowance?

A. The periodical allowance is normally paid for a period of up to three years from the date of your divorce, if the award was made after 1985. Your husband's liability ceases upon your death or if you remarry or cohabit with another partner.

Q. Can I seek an increase in periodical allowance?

A. Yes. You can ask the court to increase the award of periodical allowance if there has been a material deterioration in your financial position or a material improvement in your spouse's financial position. If, for instance, your spouse's salary increased from £15,000 per annum to £25,000, this would probably be regarded by the court as a material improvement.

Q. Can I claim a capital sum from my spouse?

A. Yes. You are normally entitled to claim up to half of the difference between the value of your net capital and the value of your spouse's net capital as at the date of your separation.

35

Q. What capital is taken into account?

A. You are entitled to make a claim against capital acquired by your spouse during the marriage. This includes any house (and furniture) acquired by your spouse prior to the marriage but with the intention of using it as the family home (i.e. acquired in contemplation of the marriage). You cannot make a claim against any other capital acquired by your spouse prior to the marriage or against any capital which was gifted to your spouse or inherited by him.

Q. What is my entitlement to furniture in the house?

A. The general rule is that you are entitled to half of all items of furniture which were bought during the marriage or in contemplation of it. As above, you have no claim on furniture bought by your spouse before the marriage or which was gifted to him or inherited by him.

Q. What should I do if I think my spouse will try to dispose of his capital to defeat my claim?

A. You are entitled to apply to the court for what is called an interim interdict against him making such a disposal. You can also attempt to freeze any money he may have in bank or building society accounts. You have to show that you have reasonable apprehension that he will act in this way.

Q. What is my position if our home was bought in our joint names?

A. You are normally entitled to half of the net value of the house as at the date of separation (no matter which one of you paid the mortgage or which one of you put down the deposit). Normally the house would be sold. Alternatively, your wife may transfer her share to you for half of the net value as at the date of separation. Accordingly, no account is taken of any increase in value between the date of separation and the date of sale or transfer.

Q. Can I reach agreement on financial claims without actually going to court?

A. Yes. You can enter into what is called a Minute of Agreement (that is, a written agreement) with your wife on matters such as capital sum, maintenance, etc. Once recorded, this is as enforceable as a court order.

Life After Divorce

Sometimes a lawyer has to do more work for his client *after* the divorce action than *during* it. This is particularly so when one partner doesn't know when to let go and continues to bother the other one after Decree of Divorce has been granted. This is often the case where one of them has met someone else and their ex-partner cannot come to terms with it. I knew of one case in which a man told his former wife that he had heard her new boyfriend was HIV positive. He continued to make such remarks and also to spend his entire lunch-hour hanging around outside her place of work. She was granted an interdict against him from behaving in this way.

Any award of maintenance for a spouse lasts for a maximum of three years from the date of divorce. It is usually the wife who makes such a claim. Sometimes she is fearful that her husband will just disappear or go abroad and as a result she will be unable to collect the maintenance from him. If these fears are well founded it is wise for her to consider accepting a lump sum from her husband in place of maintenance. I once acted for a client to whom I gave this advice. She trusted her husband to remain in this country and to make regular payment to her of the £100 per week awarded by the court. A few weeks after the divorce he disappeared to the States and she never heard from him again. If she had accepted a lump sum upon divorce she would have been considerably better off.

One of my colleagues was involved in a bitter divorce action in which the wife was seeking a huge capital sum. It soon became apparent that her husband was not as well off as she had thought and in the end she required to settle for around £5,000. Two months after the divorce her former husband won £250,000 in a 'Spot the Ball' contest. The jubilant wife bounced back into her lawyer's office thinking she could claim half of that sum. She had to be advised that it is not possible to claim a capital sum after divorce. She was less jubilant when she left.

Q. What can I do if my ex-wife bothers me by calling at my house or phoning me at work, etc?

A. You should contact the police and they will consider arresting her if a crime has been committed. You are also entitled to apply for a court order called an interdict against your former wife behaving in this way. If she fails to obey the interdict, she can be fined or even imprisoned.

Q. Does my former husband have the right to enter my house?

A. No, if the house is in your name alone. If the house

is rented in your joint names from the District Council, the Council will often agree to a transfer to your sole name after divorce.

Q. Can my former husband apply for custody of my children after divorce?

A. Yes. An application can be made to the court any time until the children are 16 if there has been a change of circumstances affecting the welfare of the children. Your former husband would require to prove that it was in the interests of the children that he have custody of them.

Q. Can an order for access to children be changed after divorce?

A. You or your ex-husband can apply to the court until the children are 16 to have the access order varied. If, for instance, your husband's visits to the children have gone well, an application can be made to the court for an increase in access. Alternatively, if the children are upset by his presence, you are entitled to apply to the court who will review the amount of access granted.

Q. Can I make a capital claim against my former husband after divorce?

A. No. You can only make a capital claim against your husband upon divorce. Once decree of divorce has been granted you can never make a claim thereafter. If, for instance, you found out after your divorce that your former husband had £10,000 hidden away in a bank account, it would be too late to make a claim against that capital.

Q. Does my former wife have any right to my estate if I die without a will?

A. No. She is entitled to nothing. In these circumstances your children would be entitled to share your estate equally among them. If you have no children, half your estate is shared between your parents and the other half among your brothers and sisters.

Q. If I have made a will in favour of my former wife, does it still stand after the divorce has gone through?

A. Yes. Accordingly, if you do not wish your former wife to inherit your estate you should make a fresh will.

Q. How long does maintenance for myself (that is, periodical allowance) last after divorce?

A. Normally for a maximum of three years if you were divorced after 1985. (If prior to 1985 there is usually no time limit.)

Q. Can I apply to the court for an increase in maintenance for myself?

A. Yes, if your financial position has materially deteriorated or that of your former husband has materially improved.

Q. Can I apply for an increase in maintenance for my children?

A. Yes, if your former husband's financial position has materially improved. However, after April 1996 the Child Support Agency (as opposed to the court) will deal with all such matters, although there will be a transitional period of one year.

Q. What are my legal rights in respect of my former husband if I remarry?

A. The only significant effect is that your former husband is no longer liable to pay you maintenance (periodical allowance) for yourself. This is also the case if you cohabit with someone else.

Q. Once divorced can I change my child's surname to my maiden name?

A. In theory, you are not entitled to change your child's name without the consent of your ex-husband. In practice, however, you can simply advise the authorities (for example, your child's school, your doctor, etc) that your child is to be known by your maiden name and they will normally accept this.

Annulment

I acted for Nasreen Akmal who was the first person in Scotland to obtain an annulment of an arranged marriage. Nasreen had been forced by her family into marrying her husband when she was only 14. She pleaded with them not to make her go through with it but they refused to listen. I did not require to go into the details of the pressure, however. All we had to prove was that Nasreen was only 14 at the time of the marriage, two years below the age of consent in Scotland. The Court of Session granted the annulment on that basis.

The court has since granted Decrees for annulment of arranged marriages on the grounds that the client was forced into it. Probably the most bizarre case was that of a man whose family insisted that he marry his cousin who lived in Pakistan. The man was in love with a girl in Glasgow and was insistent that he would marry her. His family suggested that he spend some time in Pakistan to think the whole matter over.

44

He agreed to this. When he arrived in Pakistan, however, he realised he had been deceived. His family told him that they would not allow him to return to Scotland unless he married his cousin. Among other things, they also threatened to fit him up with a crime and have him imprisoned in Pakistan. Faced with all this pressure, he gave in and married his cousin. He then flew back to Glasgow and almost immediately married his girlfriend. Once his family found out that he had entered into a second marriage, they shipped his second wife off to Pakistan. As soon as he had saved up the air fare the man flew back to Pakistan to try and find his second wife. When looking for her in her home village, members of her family actually shot at him, only narrowly missing. In fear of his life he returned to Glasgow and has not seen his second wife since. The court granted an annulment of his first marriage on the grounds that he was forced into it against his will. Ironically, his first wife had also wanted to marry someone else. It was a case in which everyone seemed to end up being married to the wrong person.

Q. What is the difference between divorce and annulment?

A. If you obtain Decree of Divorce, you are still regarded as having been a married person up to the date of the Decree. If you obtain Decree of Annulment, the marriage is wiped from the record. You are therefore regarded as never having been married.

Q. Can I obtain an annulment of my marriage on the grounds that my spouse and I have not had sexual intercourse and therefore the marriage has not been consummated?

A. No. Non-consummation of a marriage is not grounds for annulment. You might, however, have grounds for divorce if you could show that you wanted to have a sexual relationship with your spouse but your spouse refused.

Q. Can I obtain an annulment if I can prove that my spouse is incurably impotent?

A. Yes. Such an action can be brought by either party to the marriage. You would almost certainly require medical evidence of the incurable impotency. Invincible repugnance to sexual intercourse may amount to impotency.

Q. Can I obtain an annulment of marriage on the grounds that I was forced into it against my will?

A. Yes. This would normally only occur in respect of an arranged marriage. The unwilling partner would require to show that they were put under such pressure that they had no reasonable option but to go through with the marriage.

Q. What is a 'sham' marriage?

A. An example might be a marriage which was entered into purely and simply to obtain British citizenship for one of the parties. If you can show that your marriage was a sham then this is also grounds for annulment.

Q. Are there any other grounds for annulment?

A. You can obtain annulment of marriage if you can show that the marriage was not entered into under the rules of Scots law. An obvious example would be if one of the parties to the marriage was under the age of 16 at the time of the marriage. It would also be grounds for annulment if you could show that your partner was already married to someone else.

Q. Can I obtain an annulment even if I have lived with my spouse for several years?

A. Yes, although if you are basing the annulment on the fact that you were forced into the marriage against your will, this may be difficult. You should bear in mind that your spouse could thereafter apply to the court to have you declared married by what is known as 'cohabitation with habit and repute'. Your spouse would require to show that for a considerable period you were generally considered to be husband and wife.

Q. If I was born in a foreign country (for instance, Pakistan), can I obtain an annulment in Scotland?

A. Yes, if you can show that you are domiciled in Scotland. You would require to show in particular that you had the intention of remaining in Scotland.

Q. If the court grants me an annulment, am I free to remarry?

A. Yes. The court takes the view that the marriage should never have existed and, accordingly, you would be regarded as a single person who had never been married.

Q. After annulment, what are the rights of my former spouse in respect of the children of the marriage?

A. Annulment does not affect your spouse's rights in this connection. Accordingly, your spouse would be entitled to apply for access to the children and any liability to maintain them would remain.

Q. Can I claim a capital sum from my spouse in an action for annulment?

A. Yes. In this respect you are no different from a spouse who seeks a capital sum in the context of a divorce action.

Living Together

According to the statistics we keep in our office, more and more couples are opting simply to live together as an alternative to marriage. They may be put off making such a commitment by the fact that roughly one in three marriages in Scotland end in divorce. In any event, the law has slowly moved forward in the last few years to give more protection to couples who live together. If, for instance, your partner (who owns the house in which you both live) tried to throw you out, you are entitled to remain in the house for a period of six months (or longer if the court should consider an extension appropriate).

I have found that many couples are surprised by the law of joint property. I acted for one man who owned a house worth around £80,000. He had paid off the mortgage. He invited his girlfriend to live with him and after a year of cohabitation he transferred the house to their joint names. A few months later the relationship broke down and she left the house. I had to advise him that she was entitled to half of the house's value – £40,000. Had he known that, I'm sure he would not have agreed to a transfer of the house to their joint names.

I acted for another man who bought a £70,000 house in joint names with his girlfriend, with whom he intended to cohabit. He put down the deposit of £50,000 and they took out a joint mortgage for the balance of £20,000. When they split up shortly after buying the house, the man automatically assumed that once the house was sold he would be entitled to his deposit of £50,000 back. He was alarmed to be told that he and his partner were each entitled to half of the net proceeds of the sale of the house. Accordingly, his girlfriend walked away with approximately £25,000.

Sometimes one partner will try to get round the law by entering into a written agreement with the other. Indeed, some couples have entered into such an agreement prior to marriage. It is thought that such an agreement would be enforceable by law although there has never been a case in Scotland to substantiate this view. I acted for one woman whose boyfriend agreed to set up home with her (with the distant promise of marriage thereafter) provided she signed an agreement to the effect that she would have no claim on anything he owned should they split up. He wanted an inventory drawn up prior to any cohabitation (as a landlord might do with his tenant) detailing who owned what. The inventory even referred to 'six teaspoons'. My client told him that if he really loved her he would put her before any inventory and on this basis she refused to sign the agreement. She never saw him again.

I have dealt with one or two court actions for 'declarator of marriage by cohabitation with habit and repute'. They are not easy to win. You have to show that most people regarded you as a married couple. Inevitably this means that the 'wife' requires to be known by the name of her 'husband'. You also have to show that you have been together for several years and that for most of that time you were both free to marry each other. I acted for a woman who had been living with her partner for 13 years. The relationship then broke down and she wished to make a capital claim against him. I advised her that she could not do that as she was not married to him. Accordingly we raised (and won) a court action for declarator of marriage and then proceeded with a divorce action immediately thereafter. When Decree of Divorce was eventually granted she obtained a sizeable capital sum from her partner.

As far as I know, no one has ever tried to raise an action for maintenance against a partner with whom they lived but to whom they were not married. This, of course, is quite common in the USA and has colloquially been called 'palimony'. It seems reasonable that as times change and more and more couples start to live together, such a claim for maintenance should be upheld here. As a pure matter of law, however, I doubt if such a case would be successful.

Q. If I buy a house in joint names with my partner, what are my rights to it if we split up?

A. You are entitled to half of the value of the house, no matter who paid the mortgage or deposit.

Q. Can my partner put me out of a house which is rented or bought in joint names?

A. No. You are entitled to remain in the house.

Q. Can I force my partner to sell a house that was bought in joint names?

A. Yes, this can be done by way of a court action which is called division and sale.

Q. What happens if the house is bought or rented in my partner's sole name?

A. You are entitled to seek a court order allowing you to stay in the house for up to six months (or longer if the court considers such an extension appropriate).

Q. What is the law regarding the furniture in our house?

A. You are entitled to retain any furniture you bought or which was gifted to you or inherited by you.

Q. Can I ask the court to declare that I am married if I have lived a while with my partner?

A. Yes. You can raise a court action for what is known as 'declarator of marriage by cohabitation with habit and repute'. You must prove that you were regarded by most people as a married couple. (The Scottish Law Commission have suggested that the law of cohabitation and repute should be abolished.)

Q. If my partner is earning and I am not, can I claim maintenance if we split up?

A. There has never been a test case in Scotland. It is doubtful that one would succeed. It is possible in America.

Q. What is my partner's financial obligation towards the children?

A. Usually your partner must maintain the children if he or she is working. You have the same rights as a married person in this respect. You should make your claim via the Child Support Agency.

Q. Would my partner have a right of access to our children?

A. Your partner has a right to apply for a court order for access – just like a married person. Your partner would require to show the court that it is in the children's best interests that access be granted.

Q. What happens if my partner dies without a will?

A. You have no right to the estate. (If you were married you would normally have a right to the whole estate.)

Domestic Violence

Most of the divorces on the grounds of unreasonable behaviour that I have dealt with have involved instances of domestic violence. These can range from the relatively trivial to the obscene. In one case I knew of, the couple had slept in separate beds for a few months up to the date of separation. Every night, shortly before the wife was about to go to bed, her husband would pour cold water all over the sheets. In another case the husband was parked outside the family home in his car. His wife came out of the house and put her head through the open passenger window to relay a message to her husband. The message must have upset him because he pressed a button to close the automatic window thereby wedging his wife's head in the car. He then reversed the car up and down the road a few times with his wife having to run alongside. Both these women were successful in applying to the court for an interim exclusion order, resulting in their husbands having to leave the house.

The husband is not always the perpetrator of the violence. I have been involved in a few cases where the husband has obtained an interim exclusion order against the wife. In one case, in which I was acting for the wife, the husband was able to produce medical evidence to show that his wife's constant nagging and verbal abuse had caused his health to suffer to such an extent that he was on the verge of a breakdown. He was granted an interim exclusion order and his wife had to leave the house. This, however, is an extreme case. It is very difficult to obtain an interim exclusion order unless there has been violence by one partner.

Q. If I am living with my husband and he is violent to me, what can I do?

A. You are entitled to apply immediately to the court for what is known as an interim exclusion order. If this is granted, your husband must leave the house. Generally, however, the court will only grant such an order if there is alternative accommodation available for your husband.

Q. What evidence do I require to obtain an interim exclusion order?

A. The court will normally insist upon a signed statement from you, a signed statement from a witness and, if possible, a medical report confirming your health has suffered and is unlikely to improve unless your husband leaves.

Q. Is it ever possible to obtain an interim exclusion order if my husband has not actually been violent towards me?

A. Yes, although this is rare. If your husband acts intolerably (for instance, bringing other women back to the matrimonial home or causing danger to the household through being drunk) and if you have a medical report to state that your health is unlikely to improve unless he leaves, you have a reasonable chance of obtaining an interim exclusion order.

Q. Can I obtain an interim exclusion order even if the house is in my husband's name?

A. Yes. It is irrelevant whose name the house is in. Similarly, it does not matter whether your home is owned or rented.

Q. If my husband and I live apart and he is violent towards me, what can I do?

A. You can immediately apply to the court for what is called an interim interdict. This court order normally forbids your husband from assaulting you or putting you into a state of fear or alarm. If your husband is violent and threatens to enter the matrimonial home, you are entitled to apply for an interim exclusion order to keep him out.

Q. What is a Power of Arrest?

A. Your lawyer should ask the court to attach a Power of Arrest to the interim interdict. It means that if your husband breaches the order the police will usually arrest him.

Q. Will the police help me if I do not have a Power of Arrest?

A. Under our criminal law the police ought to charge your husband if they have evidence from two or more sources that he has committed the assault. Thereafter, the Procurator Fiscal has to decide if a criminal prosecution should proceed against your husband.

Q. What can I do if the police refuse or fail to arrest my husband?

A. Your only option in these circumstances is to consider proceeding with a private prosecution. However, these are very uncommon and would normally only be successful in exceptional circumstances.

Q. What do I do if my husband ignores the interim exclusion order and remains in the house?

A. Your lawyer should instruct Sheriff Officers to force your husband out of the house. They are entitled to do this under what is called a Power of Ejection.

Q. What are my rights if I am divorced from my husband?

A. Even if you are divorced, you are still entitled to apply to the court for an interim interdict against him. However, the Power of Arrest falls once you are divorced from your husband.

Q. If I am living with a violent partner but not actually married to him, can I obtain an interim exclusion order?

A. If the house is in your joint names then you have the same rights as a married woman. If the house is in your partner's name then you must first apply to the court for what is known as an Order for Occupancy Rights. These rights last for six months although this time period can be extended by the court. While you have these occupancy rights you are entitled to apply to the court for an interim exclusion order against your partner.

Access and Custody of Children

Custody battles are nearly always heartbreaking for everyone concerned, so it is important that your lawyer tells you from the start what the chances are of success; there is little point in putting a whole family through the distress of a two-year court action when the chances of success are extremely slim. There are no hard and fast rules for the court when judging these matters. However, if I were acting for a husband who had a full-time job and whose unemployed wife had had possession of the children since the date of separation, I would have to advise him that his chances of success were minimal unless he had grave allegations to make in respect of his wife's ability to look after the children – and, of course, if he could prove those allegations.

Often clients pin their hopes on an assertion that the child has a preference to be with them and that the child is prepared to declare this to the Sheriff. The trouble is that almost every parent in a custody battle makes such claims. Very often the child will tell the parent what he or she wants to hear and, indeed, there is sometimes good reason to criticise parents who put such a question to their child. I have had several cases in which my client has been adamant that their child has expressed a wish to live with them. When the child came to discuss the matter with the Sheriff in his Chambers, however, the exact opposite came out.

The court is well aware of the unhappiness children have to suffer as a result of their parents' separation, and steadfastly abides by the rule that in all such disputes it is the interests of the children which are paramount.

Once the battle for custody is over, you have to sort out the question of access. Most solicitors who deal with family law will tell you that they probably have more cases involving access disputes than any other matter. It is important to realise that the court will invariably grant access unless there is a very strong reason why it should be refused.

I had a case once in which a man was seeking access to his children for a few hours every Sunday. The only argument his ex-wife had for refusing access was that he was seeing another woman – and, indeed, she alleged that it was this relationship which had caused their marriage to break down. The court, however, did not consider there was any merit in her argument and the man was granted access. This is a good example of the court's attitude that the interests of the children are paramount. It is in the children's best interests to retain a relationship with both parents and the court therefore is not interested in the jealousies of the former husband or wife.

On a lighter note I heard of a case once in which the husband had left the matrimonial home and, finding himself virtually penniless, had built a tree hut as a temporary residence. It was his intention to seek custody of the children and, to strengthen his case, he told his solicitor that it was his intention to find a tree that was nearer to the children's school. He accepted his lawyer's advice that his chances of success were less than nil. He was granted access to his children but I understand this was on the proviso that he would not take them into the tree hut.

The terms 'husband' and 'wife' are interchangeable in this chapter.

Q. Who can claim custody of my children if my marriage breaks up?

A. Any person claiming an interest in the children. Such people can also seek access to the children. This would include grandparents, for instance.

Q. What factors does the court take into account in deciding who should have custody?

A. Many factors including satisfactory accommodation, time to devote to the children and record of being a good parent.

Q. Can the court take the child's wishes into account?

A. Yes, if the court considers that the child is old enough (normally early teens).

Q. Can maintenance be claimed from the other parent?

A. Yes, if the other parent is working or is in receipt of a reasonably high amount of benefit. It lasts until the child finishes his or her education.

Q. Is this the case even although the parent having custody is well off?

A. Yes, the obligation to maintain the child still remains.

Q. Would the other parent normally be allowed access?

A. Yes. There has to be a very strong reason before the court will refuse access.

Q. If I remarry, can my new spouse adopt the child?

A. Yes. You and your new spouse can adopt if you have the consent of your former spouse. If the court considers that this consent has been unreasonably withheld, it can dispense with this requirement.

Q. Does my former spouse have any rights if the adoption goes through?

A. No. In particular, he or she has no right of access to the child nor any obligation to maintain the child.

The Child Support Agency

I cannot remember a recent law which has caused more controversy or more distress among my clients than the Child Support Act. Many mothers contacted our firm to seek advice on the basis that the Child Support Agency (CSA) was taking months and months to collect maintenance for them. In one day alone, six fathers contacted us for advice because the amount sought by the CSA decimated their financial position.

At the end of January 1995 the Government announced some very welcome changes to the law, but it may take some time for these changes to be implemented. One of the most important amendments was that the paying parent will be left with at least 70 per cent of their net income after paying maintenance.

I act for a man whose former wife had asked the CSA to seek maintenance from him. He had a net salary of around £180 per week. The Agency sought £126 a week from him. The financial pressures became so great that he even tried to kill himself. This case threw up another huge inequity with the Child Support Act. My client had entered into an agreement with his first wife (which was ratified by the court) that she would accept a reduced amount of maintenance for the children in return for a transfer of the matrimonial home to her sole name. The CSA turned a blind eye to that agreement and insisted on the full amount of maintenance from my client. I have taken this case to the European Court of Human Rights and will argue that the Agency is in breach of the European Convention in that it is ignoring a person's right to respect for family life. One of the changes proposed by the Government is that such 'clean-break' settlements should be taken into account by the Agency in certain cases.

I have taken another case to the European Court in which our client was asked to pay so much maintenance to the CSA that he could not afford to travel to see his two children. The case therefore questions the attitude of the Agency which seems to be that it is more important for a father to maintain his children than to have contact with them. Again the changes announced by the Government, when they are eventually implemented, will help in situations such as this.

Q. Can I apply to the court for aliment?

A. No. In general, all new applications for aliment must be dealt with by the Child Support Agency.

Q. Are there any exceptions to this?

A. Yes. You can seek a top-up by the court if you are claiming a very high amount of aliment.

Q. If I seek aliment do I have to go through the CSA?

A. No. You can enter into an arrangement or agreement on aliment between yourselves. The CSA, however, has the right to override the agreement.

Q. Does it cost me anything to instruct the CSA to deal with my claim?

A. Yes. Unless you are in receipt of Income Support, Family Credit or Disability Living Allowance, you will be charged a fee of £44 for assessment of the award of aliment and £34 for collection of it, should collection be involved. The £34 collection fee is a one-off payment.

Q. If I receive Income Support, do I have to make an application for aliment to the CSA?

A. The Secretary of State will usually make such an application on your behalf even if you do not want this to happen. In this case you will not be charged the assessment or collection fee.

Q. Is it necessary to be married before the CSA will proceed with an application on my behalf for aliment?

A. No, the CSA will deal with your claim whether you are married or not. In other words, even if you never married the father of your children, the CSA can still obtain aliment from him.

Q. If I do not agree with the CSA's calculation of aliment, is there anything I can do?

A. You are entitled to lodge an appeal with a tribunal. Legal aid is not available for this, however.

Q. What can I do if I wish to increase the aliment provided by an existing court order?

A. The court will deal with this up to April 1996. After that date the CSA will deal with such matters.

Q. Is it possible for the CSA to back-date any aliment that is due?

A. No. Your former partner is only required to pay aliment from the date he receives notification of the claim from the CSA.

Q. If my husband becomes bankrupt simply in order to defeat my claim for aliment, what are my rights?

A. The award of aliment still stands during the bankruptcy. Accordingly, when he is discharged as a bankrupt you can seek from him all the arrears of aliment that have accumulated. However, he would be entitled to apply to the court to have the aliment reduced if he could show his financial position had deteriorated since the award was made.

Q. What is the position if I receive Income Support but do not co-operate with the CSA in supplying them with information about the children's father?

A. The CSA is entitled to reduce your benefit by £9.14 per week for the first 26 weeks and thereafter by £4.57 per week for the next 52 weeks.

Q. What happens if an absent father fails to co-operate with the CSA in supplying information about his financial position?

A. The CSA is entitled to make an interim assessment. Normally this is more than he would require to pay in the first instance, and therefore encourages him to co-operate.

Q. If my husband is obliged to pay aliment to the CSA, does he automatically have a right of access to my children?

A. No. Aliment and access are quite distinct matters.

Q. How are payment levels assessed?

A. The general rule is that the CSA will ascertain the father's net weekly income, deduct his rent or mortgage and half of any pension payments he makes. The sum left is called the assessable income. The CSA then uses a complex formula to work out how much aliment should be paid from this sum. Usually the aliment to be paid is approximately 50 per cent of the assessable income.

Q. Do the CSA pursue all absent fathers for aliment?

A. If the mother is receiving Income Support, the CSA will normally pursue all fathers who are financially able to pay aliment (whether the mother wants them to or not). If the mother is not in receipt of

Income Support, the CSA will only pursue the father if instructed to do so by the mother.

Children and Crime

There is much debate on child crime, particularly about whether a very young person can truly differentiate between right and wrong. The tragic James Bulger case in England helped to stoke the debate. Lawyers on the whole keep out of such discussions, which is probably just as well. Their job is not to philosophise but to help their client.

I have dealt with some cases which make you wonder about the child's awareness. One young boy, for instance, who had been a client of ours for almost a year, broke into our office one night and stole the music centre from our reception. When he was charged he wanted us to act for him and to prepare his defence. He was both disgruntled and confused when we advised him that in the circumstances we could not.

I heard of another case in which a local church had arranged a cycle run for a few less privileged youths in the area. The day was a great success and at the end of it the organisers suggested that all the participants cycle to the church to say a quick prayer and give thanks to God for giving them such a good day. While they were inside the church praying, a rival gang of boys stole their bicycles.

Q. At what age can a child be regarded as criminally responsible?

A. The age is eight. (The age in England is ten.) Accordingly, a prosecution would not be a possibility if the child was less than eight at the time of the offence.

Q. What happens if a child under the age of eight commits a criminal act?

A. It is possible for the child to be taken away from his parents on the basis that he is in need of care and, for instance, is outwith parental control.

Q. What happens if a child aged between eight and 16 commits a crime?

A. A Children's Panel will decide what to do. Sometimes, for instance, the Social Work Department will supervise the upbringing of the child. If the crime is very serious (for example, murder) then the Lord Advocate will invariably decide that the child be prosecuted, like an adult, in the criminal courts.

Q. What can the Children's Panel do with a child under 16 who has committed a crime?

A. There are three options:
   (1) no further action;
   (2) the Social Work Department can regularly check that the child is coping at home (that is, a Home Supervision Order is granted);
   (3) the child can be taken from the parents and sent to a Local Authority establishment (that is, a Residential Supervision Order is granted).

Q. What happens if a child is charged with a crime but denies it?

A. The local Sheriff will decide whether the alleged crime has been established (the word 'Guilty' is not used). If established, the case is referred back to the Children's Panel to decide what action should be taken. If not established, the case is dismissed by the Sheriff.

Q. What is the law regarding imprisonment of a child?

A. Up to the age of 16 the child can be sent to secure accommodation such as Kenmure St Mary's. If between 16 and 21 the child can be sent to a Young Offenders Institution such as Glenochil. You can only be sent to prison once you reach the age of 21.

Q. Can a child be taken into a police station for questioning?

A. Yes. There are no separate laws for the police questioning of a child. It is thought preferable that the child's parents or guardian be present.

Q. Can parents ever be charged for the criminal acts of their children?

A. No.

Q. Can parents ever be made liable for damage caused by the criminal acts of their children, for example arson?

A. No.

Q. What action can a school take if one of their pupils commits a crime?

A. The school would have the right to expel the child but normally only if the crime was committed in school.

Q. If I suspect that one of my neighbours may be abusing their child, what should I do about this?

A. If you have genuine fear for the welfare of the child you should immediately report the matter to the Social Work Department. They will investigate the situation and if necessary take the child into care if they believe that his or her welfare is in jeopardy.

Schools and Students

Whether the issue in question is discipline or bullying, the standard of teaching or the breaking of school rules, it is almost certain that some parents and teachers – and pupils – will clash over what they believe is the best for children. Sorting out such problems can often be a difficult task.

There seems to be a strange reluctance on the part of some to confront the common problem of bullying. I knew of one case in which the school, rather than tackle the bullies, arranged for the victim to work on her own in the library away from the pupils who were terrorising her. Damage to a child's health or education as a result of blatant lack of action by the school would probably entitle the parents to make a claim for compensation. You are certainly advised to report violence against your child to the police.

The general appearance or clothes worn by a pupil is another subject which can cause friction. I knew of a pupil who had very long corkscrew hair which he rarely washed. The school insisted that he have it cut (although, legally, there was little they could do). After weeks of pressure from the school the boy turned up at assembly one morning with his head completely shaved. There was nothing the school could do about that either.

Q. Am I legally obliged to send my child to school?

A. Yes. If you fail to do so without reasonable cause, you may be brought before the court. The court has the power to fine you or even imprison you. You can, however, arrange to educate your child at home, provided this is approved by the school.

Q. At what age is my child allowed to start school?

A. Between 4 years 6 months and 5 years 3 months (depending on the date of your child's birthday). They must always start in August of the year in question. It is possible to apply for an under-age admission if your child is particularly advanced.

Q. At what age is my child allowed to leave school?

A. Generally the summer leaving date or the Christmas leaving date which is nearest to the child's 16th birthday. It is possible therefore for your child to leave school at 15.

Q. If my child is expelled from school, can I appeal against this?

A. Yes, you have a right of appeal to an appeal committee which is set up by the region and is outwith the school. You have a further appeal thereafter to the Sheriff.

Q. If my child is bullied by other pupils at school, what can I do?

A. You should report the matter to the police, who may bring charges. An assault by a child of eight or over is a criminal offence, even within a school. You may also wish to complain to the school or to change school.

Q. If my child plays truant, even if it is without my knowledge, can I be taken to court?

A. Yes, you can be brought before the Education Court which is presided over by a Sheriff. You may be fined or even imprisoned. The matter may be referred to the Children's Panel if it is thought that the child's welfare might be in jeopardy.

Q. Is a teacher permitted to belt or use any other physical punishment against my child?

A. In a state school, the answer is no. You have the right to sue if physical punishment is used. Your child cannot be physically punished in a private school if either parent objects to it.

Q. If I consider that a teacher is picking on my child or is not educating my child satisfactorily, is there anything I can do?

A. You are entitled to complain to your MP or Regional Councillor or, in some situations, to the Secretary of State. You also have the right to put in a request for a move to another school.

Q. Is a teacher entitled to detain my child after school hours?

A. Probably not, but there has never been a court ruling on this point and accordingly the matter remains undecided.

Q. Do the authorities have any right to dictate what my child should wear at school?

A. A state school is entitled to expect your child to wear clothes in accordance with the school rules. Generally, though, they cannot enforce this. In a very serious case, it is possible for the child to be expelled. An example might be the wearing of a swastika. The child could not be expelled for failure to wear school uniform.

Q. Does the school have a right to dictate my child's appearance in other ways, for example, tattoos, jewellery, hairstyle, and so on?

A. Technically, your child's appearance could be a breach of school rules but it is highly unlikely in a state school that the child could justifiably be expelled.

Q. Can I object to my child receiving religious education?

A. Yes. You can withdraw your child from religious education classes. This includes a child in a denominational school who is not of that denomination.

Q. Are there any subjects which a school must teach?

A. Yes: religious education, PE and Gaelic in Gaelic-speaking areas, in addition to the normal subjects under the National Curriculum.

Q. Is there a limit to the number of pupils there should be in a class?

A. Yes. This is based on agreement with the Unions. The limit in primary schools and the first two years of secondary is 33. For the remainder of secondary it is 30. In practical classes, such as technical and science, it is 20. The number may be altered for short periods in the event of staff absences.

Q. What happens if my child is too ill or otherwise unable to sit an important exam such as Higher or Standard Grade?

A. The result can be based on the child's ordinary schoolwork. If the child sat the exam but was unwell at the time, there is a right of appeal.

Q. If the authorities threaten to close my child's school, what is the position?

A. You, as a parent, have the right to be consulted. In some cases the Secretary of State may be required to give his consent to the closure.

Q. If my parents refuse to give me the parental contribution towards my grant, what can I do?

A. Your parents are legally obliged to make payment to you. This is called aliment. You can make this claim against your parents while you remain in further education.

Q. If I spend my grant too quickly and reach my overdraft limit, how can I get help?

A. You should contact the Welfare Officer at your Student Union who will consider making an application for a payment from the Social Fund. This is called a crisis loan.

Q. If one or both of my parents become unemployed since my grant was assessed, can I then apply for a bigger grant?

A. You should write to the Grant Awarding Authority informing them of the change in your parents' financial position. They will consider a reassessment in these circumstances.

Q. Are there circumstances in which it is possible for a student to claim Income Support?

A. In some circumstances a student can claim Income Support. For instance, if you are a single parent such an application may be appropriate.

Q. If I am offered a place at a college or university but cannot find student accommodation, how do I find somewhere to live?

A. This is a very difficult situation. You should contact the Welfare Officer at your Student Union who will no doubt do everything possible to obtain accommodation for you. Alternatively, you can contact the Hamish Allan Centre, 180 Centre Street, Glasgow, who can give you assistance and advice on homelessness (Tel. 0800 838 502).

Q. If my child is to go to college or university but is only awarded a small grant, can I support him by way of a Deed of Covenant?

A. A Deed of Covenant is a binding undertaking to make periodical payments to (for instance) a church, charity or individual. The advantage of this is that the recipient is usually not taxed on these payments. Unfortunately it is not possible to obtain a Covenant for educational purposes. If you are separated you should bear in mind that your child is entitled to make a claim for maintenance, while he remains in education, against your spouse.

Writing a Will

It is human nature to avoid making a will. For many people the whole exercise comes too close to accepting their own mortality. Indeed death can be such a taboo subject that many clients make a joke about the whole thing to lighten the atmosphere. Lawyers are no better. Many of my colleagues have not made a will. It's the equivalent of dentists with decaying teeth.

Some years ago the Law Society organised a 'Wills Week'. This was a dubious concept, supposed to trigger the public into contacting their lawyers to have wills drawn up. It was backed up by a marketing campaign in many local papers and by sizeable adverts about the advantages of will-making. Normally our office is consulted by four or five clients a week seeking to have a will framed. That week we had none. Death is not easy to market.

Some of the most vitriolic cases a lawyer will come across are those among members of a family who are disputing a will. A colleague of mine had a case in which the deceased had left his entire estate to his housekeeper. The other members of the family (especially the sons and daughters) were furious. They tried to argue that their father was senile and had no idea what he was doing when he framed the will. All the evidence, however, indicated that he was as alert as a teenager. The greedy attitude of the surviving relatives led you to conclude that the deceased had made the right decision.

Q. If I die without making a will, who gets my estate?

A. If you are married your entire estate would normally go to your spouse. If you die without a spouse your estate would be shared equally among your children. If you do not have children, half of your estate is shared between your parents and the other half among your brothers and sisters. If your estate is substantial, however, the rules are different. Your spouse would be entitled to the house up to a value of £110,000, the contents of the house up to a value of £20,000, plus savings of up to £30,000. The balance would go to relatives as referred to above.

Q. Can I frame a will by myself or should I contact a solicitor?

A. You can frame a will yourself and, if you abide by all the required formalities, this will be valid. If you have any doubts you are strongly advised to contact your solicitor or the Citizens Advice Bureau.

Q. Does the will require to be recorded anywhere?

A. No. But it is advisable to keep your will in a safe place, preferably with your solicitor or your bank.

Q. Do I require to sign every page of the will?

A. Yes. Failure to do this may render the will invalid.

Q. What is the law regarding witnesses to a will?

A. Two witnesses require to sign alongside your signature on the last page of the will. It is advisable that anyone who is to be left something in your will should not be used as a witness.

Q. If I am a single parent can I specify in the will whom I would wish to have custody of my child in the event of my death?

A. You can name someone but it would not be enforceable. In the event of a court case for custody of your child, the court may, however, take into account your wishes as reflected in the will.

Q. What is the law if someone makes a will at a time when they are senile and not sure what they are doing?

A. In these circumstances it is possible to apply to the court for reduction of the will. This means asking the court to set aside the will so that it has no legal effect. It would be difficult to succeed in these circumstances unless you have medical evidence that the maker of the will was incapable of understanding what he or she was doing at the time.

Q. If a married man leaves his entire estate to his girlfriend, does his wife and children have any right to that estate?

A. Yes. The wife and the children would each have a right to a third of the moveable estate (that is, not the husband's house). The children would share their third equally among them. If the husband should die without leaving a wife, the children should share half of the moveable estate. Similarly, if the husband should die without leaving children, his wife would be entitled to half of the moveable estate.

Q. Can I change my will at any time?

A. Yes. If you simply wish something added to your will this can be done by attaching what is known as a codicil. If you wish to change the whole import of the will, on the other hand, it is best to frame a fresh will and destroy the old one. If someone were to die leaving several wills, the most recent one would take precedence.

Q. If someone leaves me money in their will how long should it usually take from the time of death until I receive payment?

A. This depends to a large extent on the complexity of the estate. If the matter is relatively straightforward then you should not have to wait more than six months to receive payment.

The Law and
Crime

Miscellaneous Crimes

As a lawyer, I have come across a number of very unusual cases concerning rape. In one case a man was charged with rape when he had sexual intercourse with a woman who was asleep. In another case a man was charged with rape when he had sex with a woman by pretending to be her husband. (The fact that she did not initially realise this makes you wonder about the closeness of her marital relationship.) Neither man was convicted of rape because it was considered by the court that in neither case was the will of the woman overcome. A statute was later passed, however, which declared that having intercourse with a married woman by pretending to be her husband was rape.

Perverting the course of justice by wasting police time has also thrown up one or two strange cases. I remember hearing of one case in which a young architect had attended an interview for a job. The interview had gone extremely well and he was reasonably confident of success. At the end of the interview his would-be employer asked if he would like a lift home. The young architect was anxious to get out of the office as quickly as possible while everything was going well. Accordingly, he made up the excuse that he had brought his bicycle and would simply cycle home. But the employer suggested that he walk with him to his bicycle and asked him where he had left it. The young architect, digging himself deeper and deeper in to the hole, said he had left it propped against the gates of the church opposite the office. When the pair of them arrived at the gates there was, of course, no bicycle there. Keeping up the façade, the young architect exclaimed (probably overacting by this stage), 'Oh my God – someone has stolen it!' The employer insisted that the pair of them then go to the police station to report the theft, which they duly did. A couple of hours later the strain of keeping up the pretence proved too much for the young man and he confessed to the police that he had made the whole thing up and had never owned a bicycle in his life. He was charged with perverting the course of justice by wasting police time.

(I never did hear the outcome of the case. It did occur to me that in the highly unlikely event of the young man receiving a short prison sentence, any period inside would have bordered on the unbearable. This is because there tends to be a hierarchy in prison where the respect you gain is to some extent dependent on how serious or 'macho' your crime. I had visions of a double murderer asking our friend over the dinner table in Barlinnie: 'What are you in for, son?', and the young man replying, 'Well, I pretended that my bicycle had been stolen . . .')

Q. What exactly is a breach of the peace?

A. You commit the offence of a breach of the peace if you act in such a way that might cause alarm to the public.

Q. Are the police entitled to charge me if I act in such a way even when there is nobody else around?

A. Yes. If, for instance, the police hear you shouting in a derelict street, they are entitled to charge you.

Q. If I am charged with a minor breach of the peace (or any less serious offence) is there any possibility that I will avoid being taken to court and will simply receive a warning from the Procurator Fiscal?

A. The police will normally report your offence to the Procurator Fiscal. It is his job to decide whether you should be taken to court. In particular he will

97

take into account whether you have any previous convictions and, of course, the seriousness of the offence. If you have no previous convictions and if the breach was not serious then there is a reasonable chance that the Procurator Fiscal would simply send you a warning letter. The letter would normally indicate that if you were to re-offend he would take that matter to court.

Q. Is it an offence to get too drunk?

A. There is a crime of being drunk and disorderly if you are so drunk as to be unable to control yourself.

Q. Do I actually have to hit someone to be guilty of an assault?

A. An assault is any attack upon the person of another. Accordingly, spitting on someone or locking someone inside a house are examples of assault.

Q. If I injure someone in the course of sporting activity, can this be regarded as assault?

A. This can be regarded as assault if you intended to injure the person or if your conduct can be regarded as reckless.

Q. What is unlawful sexual intercourse?

A. This is sexual intercourse with a female under the age of 16 but over the age of 12. (If the female is 12 or less, then the crime is rape.)

Q. What exactly is 'date rape'?

A. This is not a legal term. The normal law of rape applies whether you are on a date or not. Rape is having sexual intercourse with a woman having overcome her will. Reasonable belief that the woman was a consenting party is a defence.

Q. Is it a crime to waste the time of the police?

A. Yes. You would normally be charged in these circumstances with attempting to pervert the course of justice. If, for instance, you deliberately give the police an invented story which they then follow up, you could be charged. An example might be telling the police that you had been knocked down in a car accident (which they then investigate) when in fact you had been injured in some other way.

Q. If I am cited to attend court as a witness but refuse to answer questions put to me, is that a crime?

A. Yes, this would normally be regarded as prevarication, which is a form of contempt of court. You would usually be fined for this. If the trial in which you are appearing as a witness was in connection with a very serious offence, there is a reasonable chance that you might be given a prison sentence.

Q. If someone was to bother me by constant telephone calls, would this be a criminal offence?

A. This can be regarded as a breach of the peace. Depending on the content of the calls the person can also be charged under the Telecommunications Act (1984).

Q. If I am being pestered by an anonymous phone caller, is there anything the law can do to assist me?

A. The police are entitled to request the permission of British Telecom to trace the call. British Telecom have their own malicious calls bureau to deal with such problems. If caught, the police would normally charge the caller.

Q. If I send a cheque to someone and it does not clear, is that an offence?

A. You will be guilty of fraud if you were aware that the cheque would not clear.

Theft

There has been much discussion over the years as to what a householder is entitled to do when confronted by a burglar. Many people consider that the householder should be entitled to use any physical force in such circumstances. This is not the law. I remember a case in which two young lads broke into a house in Hamilton. While they were rummaging through the bedrooms the couple who owned the house returned home. One of the lads managed to escape by climbing out of the bedroom window (although he was later caught). The other, who was less quick-witted, hid in a cupboard in the kitchen. The wife opened the cupboard to take out a jar of coffee and found the youth standing there. She let out a yell but immediately composed herself, slammed the cupboard door shut, locked it and phoned the police. This, of course, was a reasonable action. If she had picked up a kitchen knife and stabbed the boy, this would not have been considered 'reasonable force'.

Q. If I inadvertently walk out of a shop without paying for an item, is that theft?

A. This would not be considered theft. To be guilty of theft you require to have the *intention* of stealing the item in question. It might be difficult to prove that you didn't mean to take it.

Q. In a shop or supermarket, is it possible to be charged with theft before actually leaving the premises?

A. Yes. The theft takes place when you intentionally take the item. It is a myth that you require to actually leave the shop before you can be charged.

Q. If a shopkeeper was to undercharge me and I don't tell him, is it theft to keep the balance that is due?

A. Yes. You are intentionally keeping money which you know belongs to the shopkeeper. Accordingly, you would be guilty of theft.

Q. If someone goes into a shop to steal something and her friend stays outside to keep guard, are they both equally guilty of theft?

A. Yes. Each is as guilty as the other. This is known as 'art and part' theft which means that both were acting in concert to commit the theft.

Q. If I find some lost property such as a wallet and keep it, is that theft?

A. This is known as theft by finding. In extreme circumstances you may be able to argue that the property had been abandoned by the owner, in which case you would not be guilty of theft.

Q. If I was to borrow someone else's car for an hour without telling him, is that a theft?

A. This is not considered theft as you would not have the intention to permanently deprive the owner of the car. However, it is an offence under the Road Traffic Act to take and drive away someone else's car without their permission.

Q. If on leaving a party I take somebody else's coat by mistake, is that a theft?

A. No. This is because you would have no intention to permanently deprive the owner of the coat.

Q. If I was to take money from my employers but replaced it shortly thereafter, would that still be theft?

A. Yes. It is no defence that you intended to pay back the money at a later date. Indeed, it is theft even if no one noticed at the time that the money had gone missing.

Q. If someone breaks into my house, can I use physical force against them?

A. You are entitled to use reasonable force if you consider yourself to be in imminent danger or if you have actually been assaulted by the housebreaker.

Q. If I get on a train then realise that I have lost my wallet and have no money to buy the ticket, is that theft?

A. No. You would lack the required intention for this to be a crime. If, however, you boarded a train knowing full well that you would not be able to afford to pay for the ticket, this would be regarded as a fraud.

Drugs

Lots of people wonder why the police and the courts take such harsh steps against those who commit drug offences. After all, you might argue, you should have the right to do what you want with your own body. The courts do not see it this way, however. They are aware of the multitude of social evils created by illegal drug use – whether housebreaking or prostitution to obtain money for heroin, or young people at night-clubs overdosing on ecstasy – and are determined to deter users and dealers. All the evidence points to tough sentencing for anyone convicted of supplying drugs.

It is quite common for someone who has been charged with an offence to tell his lawyer that he cannot remember a thing that happened because of the effects of drink or drugs. As you can imagine, it is never easy to prepare a defence in these circumstances. But lawyers will always advise their clients that intoxication is not a defence. Some interesting legal discussions have centred on this issue of what the law should do with someone who becomes so intoxicated or drugged up that he has no idea what he is doing and while in that state, commits a crime. The problem for the law is that you cannot be convicted of a crime unless it can be shown that you had the intention to commit it. To most people it must therefore seem a contradiction that someone who is so drugged up that they cannot form an intention can nonetheless be convicted of a crime they committed while in that state. But the law that you cannot use drugs or drink as an excuse was confirmed by the case of one man who, having drunk 20 to 25 pints of beer and taken some LSD on top of that, committed a murder. He was convicted, although a full bench of seven Judges had to sit to decide the case.

It used to be widely believed that a prison sentence would 'cure' a drug addict. They would go through the purgatory of withdrawal to begin with but would come out the other side having kicked the habit. Now, with reports that drugs are more and more accessible to prisoners, this particular form of rehabilitation may become less effective as time goes on.

Q. What is the difference between Class A and Class B drugs?

A. Class A drugs – such as cocaine, heroin, LSD and ecstasy – are regarded as highly dangerous drugs. Class B drugs are considered less dangerous, and include cannabis and amphetamines. The sentence for possession or supply of a Class A drug will invariably be much more severe than that for a Class B drug.

Q. Are any drugs legal?

A. Yes. Most drugs are legal because they have medicinal uses. Obvious exceptions include certain 'designer' drugs such as crack or ecstasy. For the vast majority of drugs it is their *possession without lawful authority* which is illegal.

Q. What is the position if someone plants drugs on me without my knowledge?

A. This is not a crime as you would not be regarded as having possession of the drugs. Possession requires both knowledge and control.

Q. If, at a party, someone offers me a drag of their joint, is that classed as 'possession of drugs'?

A. Yes.

Q. If I have a party in my house and some of my guests start taking drugs, can I be charged?

A. Yes. A crime is committed by aiding and abetting the drug-taking and, more particularly, by knowingly allowing the supply or smoking of drugs.

Q. If I borrow a friend's coat or jacket, can I be charged if it turns out that there are drugs in the pockets?

A. No. You would, however, require to take immediate steps to destroy the drugs or hand them over to the police if you found them in the pocket, otherwise you would be regarded as the person in possession.

Q. What quantity of drugs would I require to possess before I could be charged with supplying drugs?

A. Unlike certain other countries, where a minimum quantity of drugs is laid down for supply, no particular quantity is prescribed in Scotland, provided the amount is usable. It is therefore possible that a single tablet or joint would be sufficient if the circumstances of its possession indicated the intent to supply.

Q. What other evidence might the Procurator Fiscal use to attempt to prove that I possessed the drugs for the purposes of supply?

A. Supply would be suspected if the amount of drugs found on you was regarded as being excessive to personal consumption. Having the paraphernalia of supply such as scales, means of cutting and packaging quantities for sale, and amounts of cash representing the proceeds of sales would also be evidence.

Q. What are the likely sentences for drugs offences?

A. For possession of small amounts only, a prison sentence is unlikely for a first offender unless the substance is a Class A drug. For supplying drugs, a prison sentence is highly probable, ranging from three months at the lowest end of the scale, to a life sentence at the other, depending on amount, value and category of drugs.

Q. Would it make any difference to the court if I could prove that I was addicted to drugs?

A. Because of the increase in drug abuse worldwide, and the social evils created by addiction, the courts have become increasingly tough in their attitude towards addicts and are likely to view a prison sentence as a method of rehabilitation which is as good as any other.

Q. Is it a defence to any crime that I was on drugs at the time I committed an offence and had no idea what I was doing?

A. No. Self-induced intoxication is no defence in Scotland. If the taking of the drug was involuntary (for example, if someone spiked your drink), you may have a defence.

Q. What is the law concerning driving while under the influence of drugs?

A. The laws are the same as for alcohol. The minimum period of disqualification for driving under the influence of drugs would, for instance, be one year.

Being Arrested

Almost every night we receive phone calls from people who have been arrested and need legal advice. For someone who has perhaps never been arrested before, it can be a very traumatic experience. You may have no idea what your rights are and imagine that you will be locked up indefinitely awaiting your trial.

The system in Scotland is generally regarded to be very fair and workable. For instance, in some countries, you could be kept in jail for an eternity while awaiting your trial. In Scotland the longest a person can be kept for is 110 days (unless there are special circumstances). There have been many examples over the years of accused people being released because it was not possible for the Crown to arrange the trial within the required 110-day period. Such a person cannot be tried again for the same crime.

If you are questioned by the police but are not warned that anything you say may be used against you, it is unlikely that your reply can be given in evidence against you in court. There was a case in the Highlands involving three men who had been arrested for alleged rape. They were interviewed separately and all confessed to the crime. The details of all three confessions were very similar. However, the police had failed to give these men the required warning. The Appeal Court in Edinburgh took the view that the confessions were not admissible and all three were released.

The Duty Solicitor system works very well. It ensures that virtually every accused person is given the benefit of free legal advice and is represented in court at their first appearance. I once acted as Duty Solicitor for a man who was well acquainted with the cells in the Sheriff Court. He had been charged with urinating in a public close. I gave the Sheriff a fairly detailed explanation as to why the man had no other option but to do what he did. Rather than imprison him the Sheriff took a lenient view and let the man off with an admonition. The man then started shouting and swearing at me. One of the police officers later explained to me that the man had nowhere decent to stay and had hoped for a prison sentence so he might enjoy some hot food and a roof over his head for a few weeks.

**Q. If I am arrested by the police, are they obli-
ged to tell me why they are arresting me?**

A. Yes. If it is not possible for the police to advise you
at the time of the arrest, you must be told as soon
as possible thereafter.

**Q. Must the police give me a warning that any-
thing I say to them may be used in evidence
against me?**

A. No. If you are not given this warning then anything
you do say to the police may not be admissible as
evidence in court. However, if you voluntarily and
without prompting say something to the police,
that can be used in evidence in most cases.

**Q. Can I refuse to answer any questions until
my lawyer is present?**

A. The general rule is that you are not obliged to
answer any questions at all whether your lawyer is
present or not. If, however, you are detained for a
serious crime (under what is known as Section 2
Procedure) you are obliged to give your name and
address. Similarly, if you are questioned by a police
officer as a suspect or a potential witness under
Section 2 Procedure, you may require to give your
name and address.

114

Q. Is it right that I am entitled to make a phone call (for instance to my lawyer or my family)?

A. No. This is a legal myth. The police are not obliged to allow you to make a phone call although invariably they do allow this. Usually you have the right to have your solicitor informed. The police will often phone your lawyer on your behalf. Similarly, you usually have the right to have another person (usually one of your family) informed.

Q. What happens if I do not have a lawyer?

A. You should ask the police to arrange for the Duty Solicitor to call to see you. There is nearly always a Duty Solicitor on call to give advice in these situations.

Q. How long would it usually take before the Duty Solicitor calls to see me?

A. This depends to a large extent on the whereabouts of the police station in which you are detained. In a major city you would normally be visited by the Duty Solicitor within a couple of hours. In any event, if you are detained overnight and appear in court the next day, the Duty Solicitor will almost always represent you in court on that day.

Q. How long can the police detain me before they charge me?

A. Usually the police are entitled to detain you for up to six hours.

Q. What is the procedure if I am charged?

A. The police will either release you immediately upon being charged (if, for instance, the alleged crime is not too serious) or they will detain you until you appear in court – normally the next day. When you appear in court your solicitor will usually ask that you be released on bail. Bail is generally granted unless there are persuasive reasons why it should not be. One reason might be that you are already on bail or are of no fixed abode.

Q. If I am refused bail, for how long can I be detained in prison while awaiting my trial?

A. If you are charged with a serious crime (known as a Petition case) you can only be detained for 110 days. If you are charged with a less serious crime (known as a Summary case) you could only be detained for a period of 40 days. These time limits can be extended in special circumstances.

Q. Can the police stop me and then question me or search me for no good reason?

A. No. Unless you volunteer to be questioned or searched, the police are only entitled to act in this way if they have reasonable suspicion that you have committed a crime.

Compensation for Criminal Injuries

The rules regarding criminal injuries compensation were changed significantly in April 1994. Before April the victim of a violent crime was entitled to claim, among other things, any wages lost as a result of being off work due to the injuries. Now, however, the victim can only claim compensation for the injuries themselves – not for any wage loss.

This new rule can have devastating consequences. I act for a man who was stabbed in the arm at a football match. Fortunately his application was lodged before April 1994. He may be off work for a very long time and on his behalf we shall be claiming his wage loss which will amount to many thousands of pounds. I am also acting for a client who was a soldier at the time of the Lockerbie disaster and was ordered to attend the scene to help piece together and identify the dead bodies. It is difficult to think of a more harrowing task. He was given no training for this job and no counselling thereafter. He claims he is now suffering from severe post-traumatic stress disorder. However, this condition only surfaced recently and he came to see me for advice after April 1994. Unfortunately he will only be able to claim compensation for the stress from which he is suffering. He will not be able to claim for wage loss despite the fact that he may not be able to work again for several years.

The Criminal Injuries Compensation Authority (CICA), quite rightly, will invariably refuse any application if it is apparent that the victim did not report the crime to the police or failed to co-operate with the police. One reason for this is that there have been some cases over the years where applicants have been claiming for self-inflicted injuries. I heard of one case in which an applicant had apparently asked his friend to slash his face with a knife. They had agreed to split any compensation awarded. The Authority's investigations are usually so thorough that such a scam will very rarely succeed.

Q. Do I have to lodge an application with the Criminal Injuries Compensation Authority (CICA) within a certain time limit?

A. Yes. All applications must be lodged within 12 months of the crime that has been committed against you. However, the CICA does have discretion which it may well exercise in some cases of sexual abuse.

Q. What can I claim for?

A. You can claim for physical injuries, anxiety, shock or trauma which you have suffered as a result of the crime.

Q. How is this compensation calculated?

A. The CICA has bands of compensation for different injuries. This is called a tariff scheme. For instance, loss of one eye is £25,000, while concussion (lasting at least one week) is £1,500.

Q. Can I claim compensation even if the perpetrator of the crime has not been convicted?

A. Yes. Indeed, you can claim compensation even if the perpetrator has not been caught by the police.

Q. Is it necessary for me to have reported the crime to the police before I can claim compensation?

A. It would be very difficult to succeed with a claim for compensation unless you could prove that you had reported the crime to the police and that you co-operated with them in their investigation.

Q. What can I do if the CICA refuses to pay me compensation or makes an offer which I think is inadequate?

A. You are entitled to seek a review by a higher grade member of the Authority. If that review is refused you can thereafter appeal to the Criminal Injuries Compensation Appeals Panel. A member of the panel will consider whether there are sufficient grounds to grant you an appeal hearing.

Q. If my appeal fails at this hearing, are there any further steps I can take?

A. In extreme circumstances, you can ask the Court of Session in Edinburgh to review the decision. Normally, however, you would require to prove that the CICA had either made an error in law or had acted irrationally in reaching their decision.

Q. If I accept an award of compensation, can I ever go back to the CICA for more money if my health should continue to deteriorate?

A. Yes. The CICA has discretion to reopen your case after a final decision has been made if your medical condition caused by the injury has deteriorated to such an extent that your injuries are now serious enough to qualify for an award or would now qualify you for an award from a higher tariff band.

Q. Am I entitled to any interim compensation pending the outcome of my full application?

A. Yes. If your injuries are serious, the CICA will often consider making an interim payment to you if it is satisfied that your application is likely to succeed.

Q. If I have to take time off work as a result of my injuries or trauma, can I claim my wage loss from the CICA?

A. No. The rules were changed in April 1994. Now you cannot claim for any such financial losses.

Q. If I am a victim of crime while abroad, can I claim compensation?

A. You cannot make a claim under the British Criminal Injuries Compensation Scheme. If the country you were visiting had a similar scheme, you may be able to claim under that.

Q. If I am assaulted and the criminal courts order my assailant to pay me compensation, what should I do if he fails to make payment?

A. You should immediately advise the Clerk of the court in question. The court will take the necessary action against your assailant.

The Law and
Money

Debt

It is sometimes possible for an individual to arrange his affairs so it is virtually impossible to enforce payment of a debt against him. I once acted for a plumber whose business had seen better times and who was owed £500 by a joiner. It transpired that the joiner only did work for cash. He had no bank account or indeed any account of any description. He lived with his sister in a house which was rented in her name. All the contents of the house, including the furniture, belonged to her. He drove around in a van which was in the name of his brother. The only items he owned were one or two tools of his trade which, by law, cannot be taken off him. We sued him but ended up with a worthless Decree. We found out that several other creditors had sued him without success. Against the law he was bulletproof. A couple of years later I heard that one such creditor beat him up and broke three of his ribs. He explained that he was not filling in the joiner but a loophole in the law.

There are some people (usually those in business) who have a policy of waiting until the last minute before making payment of a debt. The Sheriff Officers whom I instruct told me of a case in which they were asked to take steps to enforce a decree for £5,000 against a shopkeeper. They served a charge upon him. He failed to make payment. They then proceeded with a poinding. He still refused to make payment. They then arranged a date for a warrant sale. There was still no reaction. On the day of the warrant sale the Sheriff Officers entered the shop to remove all the stock which they were entitled to sell to pay off the debt. As they were removing the baked beans from the shelves the shopkeeper was pleading with them to be sympathetic. In between sobs he explained that he had a wife and four children, that they were on the bread-line and this would finish them off. The Sheriff Officers kept replying that they were simply doing their job and acting upon the instructions of their client. When they were about to remove the last tin of soup, the shopkeeper put his hand in his pocket and pulled out £6,000 in cash to cover the debt together with any legal expenses and interest which had accrued. He must have worked out that it was more advantageous for him to keep the money until the last minute to help his cashflow. Mind you, he had to spend the rest of the morning putting all the tins back on the shelves.

Q. What can I do if someone owes me money and will not pay me?

A. You can raise an action for payment. If the sum involved is £750 or less then the action can be raised in the Small Claims Department of your local Sheriff Court without the involvement of a solicitor. The procedure is very quick and cheap. It is not always necessary to have something in writing to succeed with your action.

Q. If I am owed money by a company and the company refuses to pay me, what are my legal rights?

A. If the company has no reason for non-payment, you can apply to have it put into liquidation. Failing that, you would require to raise a court action for payment of the sums due. If you were successful you would also be entitled to most of the expenses incurred in raising such an action and interest on the sum due to you.

Q. If I am sued for a debt, what should I do?

A. If you deny the debt, you are entitled to defend the action. But you should consult your solicitor, the CAB or the Sheriff Clerk of the court in question.

Q. If I accept that I owe the debt but cannot afford to repay it, what can I do?

A. You are entitled to ask the court to allow you to pay the debt by instalments. The court will wish to see a note of your income and financial commitments.

Q. If a debt is in joint names (for instance, me and my spouse), who can the creditor sue?

A. He can sue either of you or both of you. Normally, the creditor would sue both of you and attempt to enforce payment against the one with the most money.

Q. If a debt is in the sole name of my spouse, can I be sued?

A. No. Only your spouse can be sued.

Q. What happens if I guarantee a debt?

A. You can be sued if the debtor fails to make payment. The debt therefore becomes, in effect, a joint debt. You in turn, however, can then sue the debtor for your loss.

Q. Is there anything I can do to get out of a contract with a loan shark?

A. If the contract is valid then you cannot get out of it. However, if the contract is very unfair (for instance, reference to an exorbitant interest charge against you), you are entitled to apply to the court to have the contract set aside. If you are successful the contract would then have no legal effect.

Q. If a Decree is granted against me, can my wages be arrested?

A. Yes. The creditor can continue to arrest your wages until the full debt is paid off. If the Decree is for maintenance to a child or spouse then you must be three weeks in arrears of aliment before an arrestment can begin.

Q. If a Decree is granted against me, can the creditor sell my belongings?

A. Yes, with the exception of household necessities (such as bed, cooker, etc) and tools of your trade. Any items on hire, lease or HP cannot be sold.

Q. If a Decree is granted against me, can the creditor force the sale of my house?

A. If the creditor has a security over your house (for example, your building society) then your house can be repossessed. If there is no security then the creditor would require to bankrupt you before he could force the sale of your house. (*See* MORT-GAGES, page 141.)

Q. Can I be imprisoned for not paying a debt?

A. Failure to pay child maintenance is the only debt for which you could be imprisoned.

Credit and Credit Cards

Most lawyers have at some point had to deal with a client who has gone mad with credit cards. It is possible to obtain several credit cards and spend up to the limit on all of them. I heard of one individual who took his new girlfriend on a champagne weekend to London. She was highly impressed until the bubble burst.

There was a spell in the mid-1980s when the law of bankruptcy was changed making it much easier for an individual to declare himself bankrupt and thereby have all his debts written off. This was especially useful for anyone who had run into severe financial difficulties, having run up debts on their credit cards. Many lawyers and accountants were inundated with clients seeking to make themselves bankrupt. At one point we were seeing two or three clients a week in this connection. The credit companies then became more cautious. The law has since changed again and it is now significantly more difficult for an individual to declare himself bankrupt.

Q. Is a shop entitled to refuse to accept a credit card?

A. A shop can in fact refuse to sell any item to you. Most shops, however, will accept a credit card if it displays the required symbol. (*See* SHOPPING, page 137.)

Q. Can a shop refuse to accept cash?

A. Again the shop can refuse to sell you any item. In the USA some retailers now refuse to accept cash. This is likely to happen here soon.

Q. What happens if I fail to pay back the credit company in the required time limit?

A. The credit card company can sue you for the total amount outstanding to them (unless your agreement with the company says otherwise).

Q. Is it a criminal offence to purposely exceed the credit limit?

A. Yes. This would be fraud. It is also an offence to hand over a cheque knowing that you do not have enough money in your bank account to cover it.

Q. If I go over the limit of my credit card can I immediately be sued for the total amount of credit?

A. Yes. The credit company can sue you for the total amount outstanding.

Q. Can the credit company take my card away at any time and for any reason?

A. This depends on the agreement you have with the credit company, but usually they can take your card away at any time and demand immediate repayment of any credit.

Q. If my card is stolen and I report this to the credit company, can I claim against them for any losses I incur as a result of the theft thereafter?

A. Yes. You are only liable to the extent of £50 so long as you act reasonably. To act unreasonably might include lending your card to someone else or delaying considerably in reporting the theft to the credit company.

Q. Can the credit company alter the interest charges at any time?

A. No. The credit company can *reduce* the interest

charges but cannot *increase* them without your consent.

Q. Can a credit company refuse to renew my card for no good reason?

A. Yes, unless the credit agreement specifically says otherwise. No one is automatically entitled to credit. (For instance, your bank can demand repayment of your overdraft at any time.)

Q. When I apply for a credit card, do I require to disclose any other credit cards I have?

A. No, unless you are specifically asked.

Q. Is it a good idea for me to use Switch?

A. Not really. Switch tends to be for the benefit of retailers, in that your money is immediately switched from your bank to theirs. A cheque takes a few days to clear and accordingly is more to your benefit.

Q. Is an American Express card a credit card?

A. No. Under American Express rules you have to pay when the account is sent to you (unlike Visa, for example, whereby you can pay by instalments).

Shops and Shopping

Many people come to us seeking advice about items they have bought. It is rare for these disputes to end up in court, usually because the amount of money involved is relatively small and does not merit the inconvenience and anxiety of a court case.

Nonetheless, some people have taken advantage of the Small Claims procedure (where the amount involved is £750 or less). Accordingly, I often advise clients to make use of this procedure if they feel strongly enough about the issue in question. One man explained that he had bought a pair of trousers for £50 which had shrunk dramatically when he washed them. He was determined to take his case to the Small Claims court. As he put it, 'It's not the principle, it's the money.'

Another man told me that he had bought a three-piece suit (for £29.99!) which, in the subdued light of the shop, he thought was cream. When he tried it on at home, however (in front of his whole family, he was keen to add), it turned out to be egg-yolk yellow. When his family had stopped laughing he took the suit back to the shop but they refused to give him his money back. As a matter of law, I had to advise him that they were entitled to take this stance.

Q. If I see an item in a shop window which I want to buy, can I insist that the shop sell it to me?

A. No. However, if the shop does sell you an item it must be sold at the cost specified on the price ticket.

Q. What is the law if I am short-changed in a shop?

A. You can claim the money back but it is sometimes difficult to prove. In most cases the amount of change involved is too small to merit a court action.

Q. If I buy a gift for someone (for example, a CD) and it turns out they already have it, is the shop bound to exchange it for me?

A. No. It is entirely up to the shop. Most shops will agree to an exchange if you can produce proof of purchase, such as a receipt.

Q. Is it the case that I must always produce a receipt before I can claim my money back?

A. Not necessarily, provided you can prove that you bought the item in question. For example, if you were accompanied at the time by a friend, then evidence from that friend would help. It may also be that the label on the item indicates that it could only have been bought in that particular shop.

Q. What are my rights if I buy an item which, on returning home, I notice is badly damaged?

A. You are entitled to demand your money back if you return the item in question immediately.

Q. What is my position if a shop assistant misleads me by telling me, for instance, that a garment is made of silk when it is not?

A. In these circumstances you are entitled to return the item and demand a refund of the price.

Q. What is my position if I purchase a motor vehicle which does not go?

A. If you buy from a dealer then he must repair it for you. If the fault is major, you can demand your money back. This does not apply if you buy from a private individual. 'Buyer beware' is the motto in these circumstances.

Q. If I buy an item of clothing and decide that I don't like it when I get home, can I change it?

A. You have no automatic right to this, but you may find that the shop will agree to do so purely out of goodwill, if the item is returned very quickly.

Q. What is the law if the washing instructions on a garment are wrong and I damage it as a result of following these instructions?

A. You can demand your money back. Proving the damage can sometimes be difficult, however.

Q. What happens if I buy an item on HP but I fall behind with the payments?

A. Unfortunately you are in a weak position. The HP company owns the item until you make your final payment. You should have a look at the HP agreement, which may give you protection.

Mortgages

Buying a house is one of the biggest, most expensive decisions most people ever make. Repayment of the money borrowed for the purchase – the mortgage – is usually spread over 25 years, and so can affect your spending powers for a substantial part of your life. It is vital, therefore, that you get good advice on your property and your mortgage. Your lawyer can help with both.

Even once the house is bought, however, you may still encounter some problems. When a couple split up, there are sometimes difficulties in deciding what to do about any house they jointly own. I have known many cases where the couple have agreed that such a house should be transferred to the sole name of one of them, but the bank which arranged the mortgage had refused to agree to such a transfer. This is usually because the bank is nervous that the person taking over the house will not be able to afford to pay the mortgage on their own if it was granted on the basis of the couple's joint salary. In one case in which I was involved we got round this problem by arranging for the husband (who was making the transfer) to guarantee the mortgage payments. In another case we reached an agreement with the husband on the basis that, as well as a transfer of the house, he would agree to pay £150 per week maintenance. The bank agreed to this arrangement.

One of the problems with a joint mortgage is that your partner could increase the mortgage without telling you. In the end, you are both equally liable. In one case I acted for a woman who had separated from her husband. It was proposed that their home be sold and the proceeds divided equally. On making enquiries as to how much was to be repaid to the bank it transpired that her husband had been borrowing to prop up his ailing business, unbeknown to his wife, and that the bank was intent upon repossessing the house due to non-payment of the husband's borrowing. Banks are entitled to make this finance available and rely upon the security on the house. With a joint mortgage you are both liable for all borrowings. Be careful!

Q. **For how many months would I have to be in arrears of mortgage before the building society would consider repossessing?**

A. It is unlikely that the building society would repossess unless you were at least three months in arrears.

Q. **What procedure would the building society have to follow to repossess the house?**

A. They require to send to you what is called a calling-up notice and then proceed with a court action for repossession of the house.

Q. **How long would such a procedure take?**

A. The calling-up notice allows you two months to pay the arrears. The court action, if unopposed by you, could be completed within one month. Accordingly, you would have at least three months to remain in your house and to find alternative accommodation.

Q. **If my husband and I split up can I arrange for the mortgage (as well as the house) to be transferred from joint names to my name?**

A. Yes, provided the lender is satisfied that your income can sustain the mortgage.

143

Q. If I have no savings, is it possible for me to obtain a 100 per cent mortgage?

A. In some instances lenders will provide loans up to 100 per cent of the valuation or the purchase price (whichever is the lesser). In most cases, however, building societies and banks restrict their lending to 95 per cent.

Q. If I obtain a mortgage, are there any extras I may have to pay?

A. If you borrow more than 75 per cent of the value of the house, you require to pay a mortgage indemnity premium. This is a payment made by your lender (usually a building society) to an insurance company to cover any loss the lender might incur in the event of your house being repossessed. You may also incur what is called an arrangement fee. This requires to be paid when the lender grants you a mortgage with the interest rate fixed for a set period (perhaps three or five years).

Q. Why do I need a lawyer when buying or selling a house?

A. If you buy a house with the aid of a mortgage, the lender will insist that you instruct a solicitor. This is principally because the law of buying and selling houses can be very complex, and you and the lender require to be certain that you have obtained a valid title to the property. If you do not obtain a valid title you may have grave difficulties in ever selling the property in the future.

Q. Is it possible to buy or sell without a lawyer's help?

A. This is possible provided that you have not required to take out a mortgage to buy the property (in which case, as explained above, the lender will insist that you instruct a solicitor). However, there are a great many pitfalls and you are strongly advised to use a lawyer. You should also bear in mind that because solicitors often accept personal guarantees from each other (known as Letters of Obligation) you may have difficulty in completing the conveyancing if you are not represented by a lawyer.

Q. Do I have a claim for compensation against the seller if, a few months after buying the house, the roof begins to leak?

A. Generally, no. It is therefore important that you have the property thoroughly surveyed before purchasing it. The survey should include an inspection of the roof.

Q. Can I obtain tax relief on my mortgage?

A. Yes. Tax relief is available on a mortgage of up to £30,000 at the basic rate of tax. Tax relief is only available on your main residence, not a holiday home, for example.

Q. Can I obtain a second mortgage over the house in which I live?

A. Yes, if the lender considers that you can afford it. Invariably, however, a second mortgage will only be granted either for a house improvement or to buy out the joint owner of your house (for example, your husband if you were to separate from him). Examples of house improvement include installation of central heating, double glazing, loft conversions and extensions.

Q. If I already have a mortgage, am I able to obtain a second mortgage over a separate property?

A. Usually, no. A lender is reluctant to offer a mortgage when you are committed to one elsewhere. If, for instance, you separate from your husband and wish to buy your own house, you would have to arrange for the joint mortgage over the matrimonial home to be taken out of your name.

Q. If my parents (or grandparents) want to buy their council house but cannot afford the mortgage, can I help?

A. It is possible for you to guarantee the mortgage. The mortgage would be in your parents' (or grandparents') name but you would be bound to pay it if they were unable to do so.

Q. If I agree to sell my house but the purchaser pulls out of the agreement, what is my position?

A. If 'missives' were entered into (that is, a written agreement to buy your house) then you are entitled to sue these people for all the losses you have incurred. This would include such things as advertising costs and interest on any bridging loan.

Holidays

Holidays can provide both the best and the worst time of your life. Every busy lawyer's office will inevitably have several calls during the summer months from people complaining about the purgatory they had to endure (and had to pay for). I knew of one man who had been offered a room in Greece which had no ceiling. Another booked a five-day sail down the Nile – his lifetime's ambition. He was not told, however, that his room in the bowels of the ship was the size of a large coffin. Nor was he advised that 'economy class' meant no air-conditioning. Accordingly, he spent each night lying awake in a hot pool of sweat. Needless to say, he made a claim against the travel company for misrepresentation.

One of the worst calamities that can befall a tourist is being charged with a criminal offence while abroad on holiday. I was consulted by one man who took a three-day holiday in France. Unbeknown to him, some of the English money he took with him was counterfeit, and when he attempted to exchange £300 of this money for francs, he was arrested by the French police. After being questioned for two days and nights, he was charged and kept in prison for 17 months while awaiting trial. Ten months went by before he even received a visit from his lawyer. My client spoke no French, and the lawyer who was appointed to act for him spoke no English. At the second meeting the lawyer failed to bring along an interpreter so it was equally fruitless. The trial was eventually conducted not by the lawyer but by his assistant, who knew virtually nothing about the case. The man was found guilty although the evidence against him was negligible. He wanted to appeal but was told that if he did he would require to spend another four months in prison. France is no longer on his list of holiday destinations.

Q. If I book a holiday and then have to cancel it due, for example, to illness am I entitled to a refund of any payment I have made?

A. Yes, but this may depend on the terms of your contract with the travel agent. If cancelled due to illness you would normally require a doctor's letter. The amount of the refund may depend on how late you cancel.

Q. If I incur extra expenses or suffer inconvenience as a result of a delayed flight, can I claim compensation?

A. In general not unless the travel company permits such claims. Most sets of conditions exclude them. Some travel companies pay out if the delay is in excess of a certain specified time limit. (You may have insurance cover for excessive delay.)

Q. If my hotel is not up to standard (for instance, poor meals, cockroaches in the bedroom) can I claim my money back?

A. Yes. You can sue the travel company for breach of contract or for what is called misrepresentation.

Q. If the hotel or other such accommodation is not up to standard can I sue the travel agent?

A. No. The travel agent is not liable. Your claim would be against the travel company.

Q. In which country would a court action against a travel company require to be raised?

A. In the country where the travel company has a place of business or where you live. If therefore there is a place of business in Scotland or if you live here then you can sue here.

Q. If I go abroad and get married in some romantic place is the marriage valid?

A. Yes, provided the marriage is carried out in accordance with the formalities required for marriage in the country.

Q. If the travel company goes bust, what are my rights?

A. If the travel company is what is known as 'ABTA bonded' you may make a claim against ABTA as the bond-holder. By law every travel company which offers international package holidays must be bonded in some way, although not necessarily with ABTA.

Q. If I am charged with a criminal offence abroad, the law of which country applies?

A. The law of the country where the crime was committed. That is where you would be tried.

Q. If belongings are stolen from my hotel room, can I sue the hotel?

A. This will depend on the law of the country in question. If the hotel is in Scotland you can sue. This may be limited if the hotel advertised the fact that they will not be liable for stolen belongings above a specified value. Such an advert must be in a prominent place in the hotel, usually at reception.

Q. If I am a victim of a crime while abroad, can I claim compensation?

A. You cannot make a claim under the British Criminal Injuries Compensation Scheme. If the country in question had a similar scheme you may be able to claim under that.

Q. If I am cited to attend court at a time when I will be on holiday, what is my position?

A. You must attend unless the party citing you is prepared to excuse you or if the case is adjourned.

The Law and Employment

Employers and Employees

To many people, employment law can sometimes seem very hard on the employee. This is particularly so where you have been employed for less than two years. Many people in this position have contacted me to explain that their employer has dismissed them for no apparent reason. I had to advise nearly all of them that under the law they had no right to compensation.

I have also dealt with cases where someone has left one job to take up another one. The second employer then has a change of mind and decides not to take on the person after all. The first employer has by that time taken on someone else and does not want my client back. All you can do in such circumstances is to make a claim against the second employer for what usually amounts to no more than one week's wages.

In a separate case, I acted for one man who attended an interview for a job in a grocery. He was asked at the interview if he was a smoker. He replied that he was but that he would undertake not to smoke while at work. He was given the job. After a few days at work, however, his employers told him that because he was a smoker he would have to leave. He pointed out that all the time he was at work a cigarette had not touched his lips. His employers accepted this but were insistent and dismissed him for this empty reason. It was similar to a restaurant refusing to serve a customer who had agreed not to smoke on the premises. Nonetheless, my client could not claim compensation because he had not worked at the grocery for over two years.

Even when you have worked for the same firm for two years, employment problems still arise. Constructive dismissal is one such difficult area for employees. It is never easy to win such a case. I had a client who alleged that his employer continually made disparaging remarks about his religion, remarks which were always made in private and never overheard by any witnesses. My client was forced to leave his work but the claim for compensation for constructive dismissal did not succeed.

It can also be difficult for anyone who has been accused by his employer of committing a crime and who is dismissed as a result. In these circumstances the employer does not in fact have to prove that you *did* commit the crime. All he has to prove is that he had *reasonable suspicion* that you had committed the crime. I once acted for a woman who had been accused by her employer of stealing from the shop in which she worked. The employer informed the police, who charged her with theft. The Procurator Fiscal, however, threw out the criminal case through lack of evidence. Nonetheless, her employer was able to show that he had reasonable suspicion that the alleged crime had been committed and, accordingly, the woman was not entitled to compensation.

Q. How long must I be working for an employer before I am protected against being unfairly dismissed?

A. Two years. However, if your dismissal is connected with complaints about health and safety at work or because you have asserted your statutory rights, there is no time limit. Employees have various statutory rights. One example is a right to receive a statement containing the main terms and conditions of employment. Another example is a right not to have any deduction or reduction in their wages without their consent. If an employee seeks from her employer her statutory entitlement and is dismissed as a result, then she may claim compensation for unfair dismissal. No qualifying period of service is required.

Q. If I take part-time work to help supplement my financial position but am dismissed for no good reason by my employer, what are my rights?

A. After a recent House of Lords case, part-time workers may have a right to claim unfair dismissal after two years. You can also claim any wages that were due to you including wages in lieu of notice. If the amount due to you is £750 or less, you can proceed with a Small Claims action, which is quick and cheap.

Q. What can I do if I find out someone at my work is doing the same job as me but getting more pay?

A. You can apply to an industrial tribunal. They will bring your wage up to the same rates as his if they are satisfied that both jobs are the same.

Q. What are my rights if my employer gives me a hard time for no good reason?

A. If you are hassled to the point of leaving, you are entitled to claim compensation for what is known as 'constructive dismissal'.

Q. Can I be dismissed if I refuse promotion?

A. No, but your employer could refuse to offer you future promotion.

Q. Must I be given verbal or written warnings before I can be dismissed?

A. Yes, unless the offence you have committed is a serious one, for example, theft.

Q. If I become pregnant and take time off to have my baby, must my employer keep my job open?

A. Yes, provided you have been employed for two years and you follow the correct procedures. These procedures involve you in serving a notice on your employer both before you go on maternity leave as well as before you return to work.

Q. If my wife is pregnant, are we both entitled to leave from work to look after the baby? And if so, for how long?

A. The mother is entitled to a minimum of 14 weeks' leave. During that time she is entitled to benefits but not remuneration unless her contract of employment provides for this. The father has no statutory right to such leave.

Q. What are my rights if I am sexually harassed by my employer?

A. Complain to his superior. If he does not have a superior or if the harassment continues, you are entitled to make a claim for compensation.

Q. What is my position if my employer changes my job description?

A. You can claim compensation if the change is made without your consent.

Q. If I am made redundant, how much am I entitled to?

A. If you are aged between 22 and 41, one week's wages for every year you have worked, up to 20 years. If younger than 22, half a week's wage. If older than 41, one and a half times your weekly wage.

Q. What is my position if I am offered a job and then my new employer changes his mind before I have a chance to start?

A. If you accepted his offer you are entitled to claim compensation. This amounts to the wages you would be entitled to receive during the period of notice your employer required to give you. Often, therefore, this is only one week's wage.

Q. At what age must I retire?

A. For men and women the age is 65 (following a decision by the European Court).

Entitlement to Benefits

The rules regarding who is entitled to what benefit can be extremely complex and most lawyers have difficulty keeping up with the changes in the law. To cope with these ever-changing rules, we have set up a Welfare Rights department which is run by two lawyers who specialise in this area. Any of our clients who need advice on their entitlement to benefit are referred to this department. Over the last two or three years we have found that as many as one client in three is not receiving their full entitlement to benefit. This is partly because the law is difficult to understand and also because these people have not always been advised by the authorities of their right to certain benefits.

We acted for one woman for whom we managed to obtain a backdated award of benefit totalling £8,000. Another man came to see us because he was in financial difficulties and was on a very low amount of benefit. He had outstanding electricity and phone bills and was worried he might get cut off. We asked him to call at the office again with his various bills and invoices and we agreed to write to the authorities concerned to help him out. Surprisingly, he failed to contact us. We wondered if we had said something to offend him or upset him. It was only later we found out that a few days after his visit to the office he had won almost £300,000 on the pools.

Q. What is the current rate of Income Support to which I am entitled?

A. If you are single, you should receive £45.70 per week. If you are married, you and your spouse share £71.70 per week. This is known as the couple's rate. You are first entitled to receive Income Support at the age of 16 but your entitlement may depend upon your circumstances. If you are less than 25 there is a sliding scale: if aged between 16 and 17, you get £27.50; if aged between 18 and 24, you get £36.15. If you have a child under 11 you are entitled to an extra £15.65. If the child is between 11 and 15 the extra amount is £23.00.

Q. What extras am I entitled to if I am on Income Support?

A. You are entitled to free dental care, medical prescriptions, contributions to school dinners for your children, fares to hospitals, sight tests and vouchers for spectacles.

Q. If I am in receipt of Income Support will the DSS pay my rent or my mortgage?

A. The DSS will normally pay your rent. You are entitled to Housing Benefit, which is usually paid by the authorities direct to the District Council to cover your rent. However, if you have a non-dependant living with you (for example, an aunt) it is expected that you should obtain some rent from that person. As a result, the DSS will ask you for a contribution towards your rent. If you have a private landlord you can arrange to have your rent paid directly to your bank and you would then pay your landlord from that account. Normally the DSS will pay your mortgage interest directly to the building society or bank with whom you have your mortgage.

Q. Are the DSS obliged to pay me Income Support even though I am homeless?

A. Yes. For security reasons they are usually loath to send you a Giro to an address which is not your permanent address, for example, a hostel. However, you can insist upon a personal issue Giro and can attend the DSS in person to collect your benefit.

Q. Who is entitled to receive payment from the Social Fund?

A. You are entitled to payment from the Social Fund in circumstances of extreme need. Payments are discretionary. There are three principal types of payment:

(1) Budgeting loan – this, for instance, would cover the purchase of essential furniture in an unfurnished flat. You must have been on Income Support for 26 weeks to qualify for this budgeting loan.

(2) Community Care Grant – this would cover the purchase of essential items if you have just come out of an establishment such as a homeless hostel, a hospital or a children's home and require assistance to re-enter the community. You must be receiving Income Support to qualify.

(3) Crisis Loans – this would cover a payment to you if you had suffered a fire or a flood in your house. Unlike (1) and (2) above, you do not have to be on Income Support to qualify. It also covers the situation where you may be awaiting benefit such as Income Support while your claim is being processed.

Q. Who is entitled to receive Family Credit?

A. You are entitled to Family Credit if you earn a relatively low wage, you work over 16 hours a week and have a child or children. Effectively Family Credit exists to supplement your income. For instance, a single parent earning £70 per week with three children would almost certainly qualify.

Q. What is the position regarding Unemployment Benefit?

A. You are entitled to Unemployment Benefit for 52 weeks from when you cease working. Thereafter, you will receive Income Support only. The present rate is £45.45 plus 25p Income Support per week. This is increased if you have dependants. The weekly addition for an adult dependant, for instance, is £28.05.

Q. Who can receive Invalidity Benefit?

A. You are entitled to receive this benefit if you have been off work due to illness for 28 weeks from the date of your first sick line and if you have paid sufficient National Insurance contributions. The basic rate is presently £57.60 per week. (Prior to this you may be entitled to Sickness Benefit at £43.45 per week.)

Q. What is Disability Living Allowance?

A. You may be entitled to this allowance if you are housebound or have difficulty getting around. The allowance is paid to cover the extra costs you may need to take taxis, buses, etc. or if you require help around the house.

Q. Is Disability Living Allowance the same as Attendance Allowance?

A. Attendance Allowance is appropriate if you are 65 years of age or more. The same criteria apply.

Q. Who is entitled to Sickness Benefit?

A. Sickness Benefit is paid if you can satisfy the DSS of your illness by producing medical certificates. You do not have to be in employment to receive this Benefit. You are entitled to it if you are unemployed but have medical certificates to show that you are unfit for work.

Q. Do I have to pay Council Tax if I am unemployed?

A. Yes, although the amount varies according to your circumstances. For instance, if you receive Income Support you would be expected to pay only 20 per cent of your Council Tax bill.

The Law and
Health

Your Health Rights

Most legal offices who deal with damages claims have a cabinet full of files against the medical profession. In our office we have more claims against doctors than all the other professions put together. This is partly due to the nature of the job: many professions can camouflage their mistakes, but in the medical world that is less easy.

It is often difficult to succeed with a claim for damages in respect of a doctor's alleged negligence. This is partly because it can be an uphill struggle trying to find a doctor who is prepared to give evidence against another. In addition, it is not enough simply to prove that the doctor in question made a mistake. I've come across cases where a doctor made a wrong diagnosis (resulting in the severe illness of the patient) but the claim for damages was not successful. This may sound strange to a layman – indeed, it sounds strange to some lawyers.

When a mistake is obvious, the Health Board will

171

normally settle the claim without too much of a fight. I acted for a woman who had undergone fairly routine tests at a hospital in Glasgow. On the Friday morning she received a letter informing her that she must attend the hospital urgently on the Monday morning. After a traumatic weekend during which she had not slept at all, she returned to the hospital only to be told that the letter should have been sent to another patient who had a similar name. The Health Board did not resist our claim for compensation for the stress and anxiety she had endured.

An even more obvious mistake involved another woman who attended a Glasgow hospital for a relatively minor ailment. As part of the treatment she was asked to swallow some medicine. It looked and tasted revolting but she managed to knock it back. On her way back to work she started to feel sick. She walked the streets for a while in the hope that the fresh air might help. When she eventually returned to work she was told that the hospital had telephoned with a message that she must go back there that afternoon. On arriving at the hospital she was informed that she had been given poison by mistake. She had to have her stomach pumped and was in hospital for several days. Needless to say, her claim was successful.

I heard of another case in Edinburgh in which a patient had been diagnosed as having a fatal illness. He was told by his doctor that he only had a few months to live. The man was very affluent and, upon receiving the bad news, he decided to spend all his money. Once he was penniless he was informed that the doctor had made a mistake and that he could expect to live for many years. He made a claim for all the money he had spent, but was unsuccessful.

Q. If my dentist decides to go private, can I insist that he or she continue to treat me under the National Health Scheme?

A. No. You can, however, insist upon being treated by another dentist under the National Health Scheme. The local Health Board is obliged to find such a dentist for you.

Q. Can my doctor refuse to continue to have me as a patient?

A. Yes. Your doctor does not even require to give a specific reason for the refusal.

Q. What do I do in such circumstances?

A. It is your responsibility to find another doctor. If this proves impossible, the Health Board will commission a doctor who is obliged to keep you on his or her register for a minimum of seven days.

Q. Is there any legal time limit to waiting lists for operations?

A. No. The Citizens' Charter was an attempt to reduce waiting time but you cannot sue under it. If, however, you were to suffer as a result of delay in proceeding with the operation, you might have a claim for damages against the Health Board.

Q. If my doctor makes a mistake when treating me, can I sue for compensation?

A. Not necessarily. You would require to show that your treatment fell well below the standard of care to be expected of an average doctor. An obvious mistake such as amputating the wrong leg would clearly give rise to a claim.

Q. Are schools obliged to give any form of health care?

A. The Health Board is obliged to carry out periodical inspections and in particular give injections against various illnesses. The school is obliged to provide adequate facilities for these inspections.

Q. Does the hospital have the right to discharge me from a hospital bed?

A. Yes. If necessary, they could involve the help of the police in ejecting you from the hospital.

Q. Can I refuse my child the right to an operation on religious grounds?

A. The court can intervene and order the required treatment if this is in the interests of the welfare of the child.

Q. If I am a smoker, can the hospital refuse to operate on me?

A. This has not been tested in the Scottish courts. It would probably be regarded as a matter of medical judgment. It is likely, however, that you would have the right to demand an operation if it could be shown that such an operation would probably be successful.

Q. What are my rights if I contract an illness as a result of contaminated blood from a blood transfusion?

A. If you can prove that the blood was defective you would have the right to make a claim against the Blood Transfusion Unit.

Q. If an ambulance is slow to arrive at my house and I suffer as a result, what are my rights?

A. If you can show that the delay was as a result of a blameworthy mistake, you would have the right to make a claim.

Q. If I go out for a meal and am later very sick, can I make a claim against the restaurant?

A. If you can show that the food probably caused your illness, you can make a claim against the restaurant for compensation. You should also report the restaurant to the Environmental Health Department. The result of their investigation may help your claim. In serious cases, the Procurator Fiscal can apply to the Sheriff Court for a closure order on the restaurant.

Mental Illness

Sometimes lawyers can find themselves representing a client whose mental health is questionable. A colleague of mine once acted for a woman who wished to divorce her husband because he continually accused her of being schizophrenic. These accusations greatly upset her, she explained. The lawyer noticed that while his client was sometimes highly articulate and astute, she was quite unintelligible at other times. One day she turned up for an appointment at the office wearing a balaclava. She removed it halfway through the meeting and the lawyer saw that she had shaved all her hair off and had covered her head with paint. He felt obliged to carry on with the meeting as though nothing had happened. He later advised the woman's relatives that they should have a curator appointed to manage his client's affairs.

A Power of Attorney is a useful document. It is not used where the person is suffering from mental illness but where, for instance, he is abroad or in prison. If it is not possible for someone to manage his own affairs for reasons such as these, a Power of Attorney enables a relative to do this for him. The powers it gives are wide ranging, so it is vital that you can trust the relative to whom it is granted.

Q. What can you do if one of your relatives becomes incapable of managing his own affairs?

A. You can apply to the court to have a curator appointed to manage them for him. The curator would usually be a professional contact of the relative (his accountant, for example) or a member of the relative's family. The court can give the curator certain powers, including the power to sell the relative's property.

Q. What powers would a curator have?

A. The curator can pay bills, invest money, buy items. However to buy or sell a house requires special permission of the court.

Q. What is required to convince the court that such an appointment is necessary?

A. Two up-to-date medical reports confirming incapability.

Q. Can anyone object to such an appointment?

A. The application to the court requires to be intimated to all the other relatives. They can object.

Q. What happens if a will is made by someone who was mentally unsound?

A. It can be reduced by the court if you can show that the relative did not know what he was doing when he framed it.

Q. How can I arrange for a relative to be committed to a hospital for treatment?

A. You can make an application to the court under the Mental Health Act (1984) for a relative to be detained for a maximum period of six months. The application must be accompanied by two medical recommendations.

Q. Can the relative be discharged within the six-month period?

A. The court has no power to discharge within this period but your relative's doctor may sanction home leave.

Q. If someone is detained in a mental hospital, do they have to take medication against their wishes?

A. Yes, if their doctor obtains a second opinion indicating that the treatment is likely to alleviate the illness.

Q. Can the relative's GP arrange for committal against the family's wishes?

A. Yes, but the court must hear the family's point of view before making the order.

Q. Can someone register themselves into a mental hospital?

A. Yes, on a voluntary basis. If the hospital refuse to take the person on a voluntary basis then a member of the family or the person's doctor must make an application.

Q. What is a Power of Attorney?

A. This is a document which allows one relative to act for another but not due to mental illness. It is appropriate where, for instance, the relative is in prison or abroad.

Industrial Deafness

Some insurance companies have quite stringent rules when dealing with industrial deafness claims. In particular, they may argue that your case is time-barred if they feel that you ought to have known, more than three years ago, that your deafness was linked to conditions at work. If the insurance company refuses to settle your claim, you can encounter difficulties in taking the case further. Such court actions for damages can be frighteningly expensive and most people could not contemplate raising such an action without the benefit of legal aid. But it is often difficult to obtain legal aid for a case such as this as the Legal Aid Board will not grant assistance if it feels that the amount of compensation involved is relatively small. Often claims for industrial deafness do not amount to much more than £2,000 and the Board may regard that as too little to merit legal aid. If your claim is worth £750 or less then this would be regarded as a small claim, and legal aid is never granted for such amounts. However, the procedure for a small claim action is very cheap and straightforward and I've had many clients who have successfully conducted such actions by themselves. Even if you were to lose, any expenses would be fairly minimal.

Most Ear, Nose and Throat consultants will tell you that they have come across people who have falsely claimed to be deaf. As experts, they can of course easily see through this: such claimants will often start off by answering all the consultant's questions with the word 'Pardon?', and it is only when they are told that their trousers are on fire that they suddenly regain their hearing. The respect shown to these consultants is such that, almost without exception, the insurance company will accept the terms of their report.

Q. If it transpires that I started to suffer from deafness as a result of noise at work back in the 1960s, is that too long ago for me to have a claim?

A. You are entitled to claim for industrial deafness if the noise started on or after 1 January 1963, so long as your claim is not time-barred as referred to in the question below.

Q. If I have suffered from industrial deafness for more than three years, am I too late to make a claim?

A. Normally you would require to make a claim within three years of being told by a doctor or an Ear, Nose and Throat specialist that your hearing loss is noise-related, otherwise your claim may be time-barred.

Q. How deaf do I have to be before I have a claim?

A. The level of hearing loss must usually be confirmed by an Ear, Nose and Throat consultant. It is on the basis of such a report that you would be advised whether or not a claim was worth pursuing.

Q. Is there a scheme for calculating how much compensation I am entitled to which is linked to the extent of my deafness?

A. The level of compensation awarded is dependent on two main factors: your age and your decibel loss. The latter should be confirmed in your medical report.

Q. If I have had several employers over the years, which one am I supposed to sue?

A. You would require to claim against all your previous employers whom you consider exposed you to excessive noise.

Q. What happens if I make a claim against my former employers but they refuse to pay up?

A. If your former employers refused to settle the claim then your only option would be to raise a court action. This could normally be raised in the local Sheriff Court.

Q. If, to back up my claim, I require documentation from my previous employers and they fail to produce it, what can I do?

A. It may help you to apply to the DSS, Contributions Agency, Longbenton, Newcastle upon Tyne. For a fixed fee they can supply you with a history of your employment.

Q. If the company where I used to work no longer exists, is this a problem?

A. This should not normally be a problem if you are able to ascertain the name and address of the insurance company who act for your former employers. A claim can be made to that insurance company.

Q. If I receive a sum in compensation for industrial deafness and my deafness thereafter becomes worse, can I seek an increase in the compensation?

A. Whenever an insurance company makes payment of compensation they invariably ask that you sign a discharge giving up any further rights you have to claim in respect of your noise-induced deafness. If you signed such a discharge, no further claim can be made.

Q. If I consult my lawyer for help, do her fees come off my compensation or does the insurance company pay her separately?

A. If your claim is successful then normally the insurance company will pay your solicitor's fees. If unsuccessful, you would require to pay these fees, but you may be covered by legal aid.

The Law and Cars

Buying and Selling Cars

Our office receives a great number of calls on the question of buying and selling cars. The majority of problems seem to occur where a car is bought from a private individual – that is, through a small ad in the paper, for example, not from a dealer. If you buy a car in this way, it is always advisable to ask a mechanic or a friend who knows about cars to inspect the vehicle before you go ahead with the purchase. I knew of one man who bought a car from someone in a neighbouring street. While driving back to his own house less than half a mile away, the car caught fire. The man could not claim his money back, however, because the seller had not actually told him any lies.

It is useful to know that if you purchase a car on HP and it turns out to have a material defect, you can demand repayment from the HP company. In one case I heard of, a man purchased a car from his local garage. A couple of days later the brakes failed and he nearly ran over a pedestrian. The garage agreed to his demands for his money back but continually delayed repayment. Eventually, the garage went bust and the man thought he could say goodbye to his money forever. His lawyer was able to advise him that his claim should have been directed against the HP company who, fortunately, paid up without difficulty.

Q. What is my position if I buy a car from a private individual (or at an auction) and it turns out to have a material defect, such as faulty brakes?

A. Buyer beware! You have no right against a private seller unless you can prove that the seller has lied to you, for example saying that the brakes have just been repaired.

Q. What is my position if I buy a car from a dealer which turns out to have a material defect?

A. You are entitled to demand your money back. You are not entitled to demand a replacement car although the dealer may offer you one. You are not obliged to accept a replacement car.

Q. What is my position if I purchase a car from a dealer and a significant defect emerges some months later (outwith the time of the guarantee)?

A. You have a right to demand compensation for the cost of the repair that is required to the car provided that the defect was not simply due to wear and tear.

Q. If I hand in my car for a repair and I do not pay the garage, can the garage retain my car?

A. Yes. They have what is known as a right of lien – provided they have actually carried out repairs to the car.

Q. If I hand my car into a garage to carry out a repair and they fail to do it satisfactorily, do I require to give them another chance to repair it?

A. No. You are entitled to have the repair carried out elsewhere. However, for your own convenience, you may prefer to give the garage a second chance to make the repair to your satisfaction.

Q. What happens if I buy a car on HP and fail to pay the HP payments?

191

A. The HP company virtually always has the right to repossess the car.

Q. If I purchase a car on HP which turns out to have a material defect, who should I sue?

A. You are only entitled to sue the HP company.

Q. If I buy a car and it turns out to be subject to HP, can I keep the car?

A. Yes, provided you are a private purchaser and you had no knowledge of the HP agreement.

Q. If I buy a car which turns out to be 'on hire', can I keep it?

A. No. In these circumstances, you must return the car to the hire company. You are entitled to reclaim the purchase price from the person from whom you bought the car.

Q. If I buy a car which has no safety belts in the back seat, am I obliged to have these fitted?

A. No, but where safety belts are fitted it is an offence not to use them. You can be fined up to £100 for this.

Road Accidents

The general law regarding road accidents is that a driver has a duty of care towards other road users. Sometimes that duty can be breached in spectacular fashion. I recall a case where a driver missed the turn-off on a motorway. He decided to reverse back towards the junction, inevitably causing an accident. I have also heard some bizarre excuses from people accused of causing road accidents. A favourite excuse is to declare that the brakes failed. The police invariably investigate such claims and it almost always turns out that there was nothing wrong with the brakes at all.

It can be difficult for lawyers, insurance companies or even doctors to be entirely accurate in their assessment of the pain suffered by the victim of a road accident. A colleague told me of a case in which his client had suffered a back injury in a fairly serious road accident. Every time he went to see his lawyer it would take him five minutes to climb the stairs to the office and almost as long again to sit down in the seat provided. Throughout each meeting his face was contorted with pain and every sentence he uttered began with 'The back is bad today'. Everyone was convinced of the man's suffering and the negligent driver's insurance company paid out around £6,000 for his injury. A few days later, purely by chance, his lawyer saw him running for a bus at such a speed that he might have overtaken an Olympic sprinter.

Q. If I am injured in a road accident caused by someone else, can I claim for this?

A. Yes. You can claim compensation for pain, suffering and disability caused by the accident and for certain other losses such as wage loss.

Q. So if I am off work as a result of my injury, I can claim my wage loss from the other driver's insurance company?

A. Yes, but there may be a deduction in respect of benefits you received while off work.

Q. How much compensation am I entitled to for my injury?

A. It depends on the extent of the injury. A typical whiplash injury might merit between £1,500 and £3,000. A broken leg could be in the region of £4,000. (Compensation in Scotland is much lower than in many other countries such as the USA and Eire.)

Q. Who pays for damage to my car if I am comprehensively insured?

A. Your own insurance company will pay for the damage regardless of who caused the accident. You would still require to pay the excess on your insurance policy, however. (If the other driver caused the accident you can claim this excess from his insurance company.)

Q. Who pays for damage to my car if I have third party insurance?

A. The insurance company for the other driver if the accident was caused by that driver.

Q. If I am insured third party and my car is off the road being repaired as a result of the accident, will the other driver's insurance company cover the cost of my hiring another car?

A. Yes, they should do so if reasonable means of public transport are not available to you. Be aware that you are liable in the first instance to the car hire company and may have to pay them long before your claim is eventually settled.

Q. If I am not insured, can I still make a claim against the insurance company of the driver who caused the accident?

A. Yes, whether or not you are insured is irrelevant to your claim. Of course, the police may still charge you with driving the car without insurance.

Q. If it transpires that the driver who caused the accident is not insured, what do I do?

A. You would require to make a claim against him personally. Often such a driver (for example, a joyrider) has no money. In such circumstances you can make a claim for your injury against the Motor Insurers Bureau.

Q. If I consult a solicitor, who pays his costs?

A. If the claim is for more than £750 then the other driver's insurance company usually pays your solicitor's costs – but only if your claim is successful.

Q. **If I suffer distress and anxiety as a result of witnessing an accident, can I claim compensation from the insurance company of the driver who caused it?**

A. Yes, you may have a claim even though you were not actually hurt. Normally, however, the person whose injury you witnessed would have to have some connection with you, such as a friend or a relative.

Q. **If the insurance company refuses to make payment of compensation what should I do?**

A. You are entitled to raise a court action and to claim interest on the sum you are seeking.

Road Traffic Law

Many clients seem quite unaware of several road traffic laws. This is not necessarily their fault. It is often the case that they have never had an opportunity to learn what the law is. I once acted for a man who could not afford an MOT test for his car. He decided simply to leave his car parked outside his house, which was situated in a quiet cul-de-sac. His plan was to save up over two or three months and then submit his car for the MOT test. When the police charged him with having no MOT certificate he told me that he genuinely had no idea that it was an offence to leave such a car parked outside your house. Ignorance of the law, of course, is no defence.

I have been asked by drivers how much they can drink without breaking the law. My advice has always been to take no alcohol at all. Although the prescribed limit is three units of alcohol, we have all felt the effects of a lunch-time glass of wine or beer, especially on an empty stomach. Many people feel it should be an offence to drive when you have *any* alcohol in your system. The court will sometimes invoke a very serious penalty for drink driving. I was involved in one case where a man was charged with driving with twice the prescribed amount of alcohol in his system. Even though it was his first offence the Sheriff sentenced him to three months in prison. He appealed but the High Court of Appeal upheld the sentence.

Q. How many penalty points must there be on my licence before I can be disqualified?

A. You are disqualified on reaching 12 points within a three-year period. Upon disqualification the points are wiped out.

Q. Will I automatically be disqualified if I am convicted of drunk driving?

A. Yes, except in a case of 'special reason', such as an extreme medical emergency.

Q. How much alcohol could I take without failing a breath test?

A. To be safe, take none! The authorities indicate the prescribed limit is reached within three units of alcohol (for example three small spirits or three half pints of normal strength beer).

Q. If I fail a breath test on the way to work as a result of alcohol I had drunk the night before, am I still guilty?

A. Yes. This highlights the dangers of drinking and driving at any time.

Q. Can I refuse to take a breathalyser test if the police stop me?

A. You can refuse, but if you have no good reason for refusal you can be charged with the offence of failing to provide a breath sample. The penalties for refusing a breath test and the penalties for taking such a test and failing it are usually the same. Accordingly, there is no advantage in such refusal.

Q. If I have too much to drink and decide to sleep it off in my car, can I be charged?

A. Yes, if you are in the driver's seat. You can even be disqualified. Charges are unlikely if you are in the back seat.

Q. What is the likely outcome if I am stopped for speeding?

A. Three penalty points on your licence and a fine linked to the amount of the speed. You can be disqualified if the speed is excessive (for example, over 100mph).

Q. If I am charged with driving at a very high speed, can this be regarded as 'dangerous driving'?

A. Such a speed (over 100mph, for instance) may attract a charge of dangerous driving which carries a compulsory disqualification of twelve months with an added requirement to re-sit a test of competence to drive thereafter.

Q. If I am stopped by only one policeman, is he entitled to charge me with a road traffic offence?

A. Most serious offences require the presence of two police officers but some of the lesser ones do not (for example non-compliance with a road sign). Under a recent law, road traffic convictions can also follow on evidence from static cameras.

Q. If I forget to renew my licence, what happens?

A. You will normally be punished by a fine and two penalty points. Remember that you are not usually covered by insurance if your licence has expired.

Q. If my car is untaxed or uninsured or has no MOT, can I leave it parked outside my house?

A. No, this would be an offence. You would require to leave it in a private place, such as your driveway or garage.

Q. What is the position if my car passes an MOT test but shortly afterwards the police charge me with having faulty tyres, brakes or exhaust? Is this a defence in court?

A. This is not a defence, but you should advise the court of the circumstances as this should mitigate any penalty the court might impose. You would probably have a claim against the garage for any losses you incurred as a result of their negligence (for instance, you could claim back any fine imposed against you).

Q. If I simply forget to renew my MOT, what is my position?

A. This is an offence. A fine will follow but no penalty points will be imposed.

Q. If my employer asks me to drive his car and it transpires I am not insured to drive it, what happens?

A. You are not guilty of an offence provided you neither knew nor had reason to believe there was no insurance.

The Law and Your Rights

Accommodation Rights

Many people come to us seeking advice about problems with rented accommodation. Some of their fears are unfounded because there are many laws which protect the rights of those who rent flats or houses from private landlords or the Council.

We acted for a woman whose rented flat turned out to have a leaking ceiling. She had to spend most of the time with half a dozen buckets and basins on the floor to catch the drips. Despite her complaints, though, the owner of the flat was very slow to act. We advised her that all landlords are obliged to keep their accommodation 'wind and water-tight', and that as hers was obviously failing in this duty, she was entitled to hold back a proportion of her rent until the repairs were carried out. This was enough to spur her landlord into action.

I heard of a student who had been threatened with eviction because his neighbours complained he continually played loud heavy metal music. He was advised by his lawyer that his landlord would have to serve a 'notice to quit' before any court action could begin. The lawyer went on to explain that the student could ask for the court action to be frozen for two to three months while he applied for legal aid. He had worked out that by that time the summer term would be over and he would be out the flat anyway. Faced with these legal difficulties, the landlord gave in and let the student stay until the end of the term.

Q. If I fall behind with my rent, can my landlord evict me?

A. Your landlord can only evict you once he has served upon you what is known as a notice to quit, which gives you at least 28 days notice of eviction. Once he has served this notice to quit he must then obtain a court order to evict you. It would normally take your landlord some weeks to obtain and enforce such a court order. If your rent is brought up to date in the meantime, it would be difficult for your landlord to succeed in evicting you.

Q. Can I be evicted from my Council flat if I allow my boyfriend to stay overnight regularly?

A. The Council are not entitled to take any action even if your boyfriend is living with you. (It does not follow, however, that he can take over the tenancy if anything should happen to you.)

Q. If I share a flat with fellow students and the neighbours complain that we make too much noise or the landlady accuses us of breaking items of furniture, can we be evicted?

A. Your landlady would have to obtain a court order to evict you. If you defend the action, it is up to the court to decide whether your behaviour is such as to merit eviction. The landlady would require to show that the damage to the property and the noise was such that it is reasonable for her to evict you.

Q. Is my landlord responsible for paying the Council Tax on my flat?

A. Usually, no. This is generally regarded as a personal tax upon you, the occupier. One exception is if you live in a house in multiple occupation (for instance, a house containing several bedsits, one of which you occupy). In these circumstances the landlord is liable.

Q. **If my landlady provides my flat with a television, who is responsible for paying the TV licence?**

A. The tenant is responsible as the user of the TV set. This is the case even if the TV is provided by the landlady.

Q. **What is my position if my landlord refuses to refund my deposit when I move out?**

A. If he has no good reason to refuse to refund the deposit, you should sue him for this amount. If the amount is £750 or less, you can sue him under the Small Claims Procedure in your local Sheriff Court.

Q. **What is the law regarding squatters?**

A. Squatters have no legal rights in Scotland. However, a court order must be obtained before they can be removed from any premises in which they squat.

Q. **If a major repair is required (for instance, if my gas fire starts to leak), can I insist that the landlord take steps to repair it?**

A. The landlord is usually obliged to carry out any important repairs of this type.

Q. If I take in a lodger who is on Income Support, can I get a reduction in my Council Tax?

A. No. However, if by taking in a lodger you lose your rebate for what is called one-person sole residence, you are entitled to claim Council Tax Benefit. This benefit can be up to 25 per cent of your Council Tax.

Q. If my neighbour puts down rat poison in his garage and I am worried about the health risks, is there anything I can do about this?

A. By and large, your neighbour is entitled to act in this way within the confines of his own premises. If his actions constitute a danger to the public health, however, you could report the matter to the Environmental Health Department.

Q. If a construction firm begins work near my house at 7.30 a.m., thereby waking me up, can I do anything about this?

A. It is possible for you to apply to the court for a court order called an interim interdict against the work being carried out at that time in the morning. You would require to show that it was unreasonable and unnecessary for the work to be done so early in the day.

211

Negligence

The general rule in Scotland is that you can make a claim for compensation against someone if you can prove that you have suffered as a result of their negligence. One of the most famous cases in Scotland is on this very point. A woman bought a ginger beer and, upon drinking it, noticed a snail in the bottle. She was entitled to compensation from the manufacturers for the illness and upset she suffered.

I have come across some bizarre negligence claims in my time as a lawyer, none more so than that of one man who wished to raise an action against an oil company. He claimed that while working on one of their North Sea oil-rigs he had slipped on some oil and broken his leg. When I asked him what his job on the oil-rig consisted of, he explained (without embarrassment) that he was employed to clean up any spilt oil. I advised him that because his case was so weak, the chances of obtaining legal aid (which he needed to proceed with his action) were virtually nil. He insisted that I lodge an application, however – and, unbelievably, a legal aid certificate was granted.

I proceeded with the court action and remember our Counsel saying that although he was prepared to fight the case it was probably the worst he had ever come across, and that any offer of compensation from the oil company should be accepted. To make matters even worse, our client's only witness then died. Counsel was even more adamant that all attempts to settle the case should be made.

Shortly before the day of the final hearing, the oil company offered £1,000. Against our advice, our client refused to accept. The day before the hearing, they increased their offer to £1,500 – but this, too, our client rejected. On the actual morning of the hearing the oil company raised the figure to an incredible £6,000. We told our client that if he refused our advice to take this offer, we would have to withdraw from acting for him. He grudgingly agreed, while muttering that our initial advice to accept the two previous offers had obviously been wrong.

Counsel and I were bemused as to why the oil company had increased their offer so dramatically. It was only later that we found out that their two principal witnesses were by then working in Indonesia and that it would have cost so much to fly them to Edinburgh that it was in fact cheaper to settle the case at £6,000. (Of course, if our client had not obtained legal aid in the first place, he could not have afforded a court action – and therefore would not have received a penny.)

It is apparently the case that the majority of people who are involved in accidents do not realise that they have a claim for compensation against whoever caused the accident. Statistics show that perhaps only one out of ten people proceed with such a claim. This is probably because little attempt has been made to broadcast people's rights in this area of law.

Q. Can I claim compensation if I suffer financial loss because the train I am travelling on is seriously delayed due to the negligence of the operator?

A. You may be able to claim compensation provided you can prove that the delay was caused by the fault of the operator.

Q. If I ask a jeweller to fit a battery in my watch and, while doing so, he damages the watch beyond repair, is there anything I can do?

A. If the damage to the watch was caused by the jeweller's negligence, you are entitled to compensation equivalent to the value of the watch (not the cost of replacement).

Q. If I take my jacket to the dry-cleaners and it comes back damaged, can I insist that the dry-cleaners replace it?

A. Assuming that the damage was caused by the negligence of the dry-cleaners, they are obliged to repay you the value of the jacket (not the cost of replacement). However, they may be able to escape liability if there is a notice in the shop, in a prominent place, specifically stating that you hand clothes in for cleaning at your own risk. Such a notice would probably be valid if it was regarded as fair and reasonable.

Q. If an airline loses my luggage, am I entitled to compensation for the inconvenience?

A. You may be entitled to claim compensation if you can prove that the loss of the luggage was due to the fault of the airline company. Such compensation would probably be minimal, though.

Q. If I am wrongly accused of shoplifting, can I demand compensation from the shop?

A. You may be entitled to make a claim for compensation if you could show that the shop had no reasonable cause for believing that you had committed a shoplifting offence.

Q. What can I do if a photo lab ruins my negatives or prints?

A. You are entitled to have your negatives processed with professional care and skill and, if that was lacking, you are entitled to make a claim for compensation for loss of the photographs. The compensation involved would normally be minimal. However, it might be more if you could prove that the photographs were of sentimental value, for example, wedding photographs.

Q. If I suffer stress and strain at work, can I make a claim for compensation against my employers?

A. This has never been tested in the Scottish courts. It is possible that such a claim would be successful if you could show that your employer's system of work was unreasonable and likely to result in strain or stress.

Q. If I suffer injury to my health through passive smoking at work, do I have a claim against my employers?

A. Compensation has been paid in England in an out-of-court settlement in a case such as this. It has never been tested in Scotland but such a claim might succeed if you could show that your employers took no reasonable steps to protect you from the alleged dangers of passive smoking.

Q. If I damage my car as a result of driving over a large hole in the road, do I have a claim against the Council?

A. You would be entitled to make a claim for compensation if you could show that the Council knew or ought to have known about the existence of the hole and that they failed to take steps to have the hole repaired within a reasonable time. You may also have a claim if you could prove that the Council caused the hole.

Q. If a newspaper prints a story about me which is untrue, what can I do?

A. You are entitled to make a claim for compensation for defamation. One difficulty is that legal aid is not available for actions of defamation.

Q. If I suffer an accident while on university premises (for instance, if I slip on a spilled drink at the Student Union), can I claim compensation?

A. If you can prove that the Union had no reasonable system for keeping the floors clean and safe, then you would be entitled to make a claim for compensation.

Q. If my child is injured while playing in a Local Authority park (falling on broken glass, for instance), do I have a claim for compensation?

A. You would probably have a claim for compensation if you could show that the Local Authority had failed in its duty to take reasonable steps to inspect the park for such dangers or to maintain the park to a reasonable standard.

Q. If I send a package through the mail and it does not arrive, do I have a claim against the Post Office?

A. If you can show that the package was sent by registered post then the Post Office would normally be liable to make payment to you of compensation, unless the Post Office could show that it had not acted negligently. If you can show that the package was posted (although not by registered post) then the Post Office may be liable to pay you a minimal amount of compensation.

Q. Do I have a claim if, while playing golf, I am hit by a stray golf ball and if the player in question failed to shout 'Fore'?

A. If you can prove that the other player failed to shout 'Fore' then you may have a claim against him for any injuries you have suffered. You would probably also have to show that the player knew the ball was heading in your direction.

General Points

Q. If I am scared of being mugged at night, am I entitled to carry an anti-attacker spray?

A. No. They are illegal in this country, although permissible in the USA and parts of Europe. In Scotland, they would come under the definition of offensive weapons. You are entitled to carry a personal alarm unit which can emit a high-pitched screeching noise. You might also be entitled to spray an attacker's eyes with, for instance, perfume, provided you could prove that your actions were in self-defence.

Q. If I witness a crime, such as an assault, can I give evidence but remain anonymous?

A. You would require to give evidence in court and unfortunately therefore you cannot remain anonymous. But you are entitled to state your address as care of the police so that no one will know where you live.

Q. What would happen to me if I did not fill in the Census?

A. If you fail to fill in the Census you can be prosecuted and fined.

Q. Can I be prosecuted for failing to register on the Voters Roll?

A. You can be prosecuted and fined for failing to comply with or giving false information to the Registration Officer who compiles the Voters Roll.

Q. Can I be fined for not having a dog licence?

A. No. Since 1988 there is no longer a requirement to obtain a dog licence.

Q. At what age can you leave a child unattended in your house?

A. The law does not in fact specify an age, but you require to show the reasonable care of a reasonable parent. In practice, however, the police will generally regard it as an offence if the child is under 16.

Q. Does a father have the right to prevent a mother proceeding with an abortion?

A. There has not been a test case in Scotland but in the light of decisions in other countries the answer is probably no.

Legal Aid

Civil Legal Aid

It is becoming more and more difficult to qualify financially for civil legal aid. In many instances you can now only afford to go to court if you are either very poor (and therefore manage to obtain legal aid) or if you are very rich (and can pay your legal fees). This is a huge impediment to justice and it can only be hoped that at some point the rules regarding eligibility will be relaxed.

The contribution system is also far from perfect. I recently had a case in which a woman asked me to apply for legal aid to raise an action for damages against one of the world's largest companies. She earned around £160 net per week but was asked for a contribution of almost £1,500 towards the cost of the case. It was inconceivable that she could pay this. Another client on low, part-time earnings asked me to apply for legal aid to go to court to seek an increase in the maintenance paid to her by her former husband in respect of her two children. The Legal Aid Board asked for a contribution of around £1,000. The reason she came to me in the first place was because her financial position was dire and she simply could not make ends meet. How the Board expected her to pay a huge legal aid contribution, thereby making her financial position even worse, is beyond comprehension.

Q. Can I obtain legal aid simply for advice or is it only granted to cover a court action?

A. You can obtain legal aid for advice. This is called 'legal advice and assistance'. It simply involves signing a form in your lawyer's office.

Q. Who qualifies for free legal advice and assistance?

A. People on Income Support, Family Credit benefit or those earning less than £63 per week net (after certain allowances for dependants) qualify for free legal advice and assistance. However, you must also qualify on capital (see below).

Q. Does the Legal Aid Board take into account any capital I have?

226

A. Yes. You will not qualify for advice and assistance if you have capital of £1,000 or more. However, the Board again takes into account any dependants you may have. If, for instance, you have a wife and two children, your capital limit is £1,635. There are also certain higher exemptions for people over retirement age.

Q. What is the position if I earn more than £63 per week?

A. If you are a single person and earn more than £63 net per week but less than £154 net per week you are entitled to advice and assistance. This is subject to a contribution by you to the Legal Aid Board. These figures will be higher if you have dependants (but any income or capital of your spouse is taken into account).

Q. How many times can I visit my lawyer under advice and assistance?

A. The Legal Aid Board puts a limit on the amount of work your lawyer is entitled to do for you. Normally it would cover at least three or four meetings with your lawyer.

Q. What do I do if I want to raise a court action?

A. You require to apply to the Legal Aid Board for a Legal Aid Certificate. As with advice and assistance the scheme works on a contribution basis but the Legal Aid Board looks at your financial position in greater detail. In particular, if you are working, it will ask your employer to fill in and sign a form confirming your earnings.

Q. To obtain such a Legal Aid Certificate do I require to show the Legal Aid Board that I have a good case?

A. Yes. You require to produce evidence to the Board (statements, documentation and so on) which indicates that you have reasonable prospects of success.

Q. Are there any types of case which legal aid does not cover?

A. Yes. These include cases of defamation, small claims actions (i.e., cases worth less than £750) and representation by your solicitor at an industrial tribunal or DSS appeal.

Q. If I win my case and receive a sum of money as a result, can the Legal Aid Board deduct

from that sum the amount it has paid out to my lawyers?

A. Yes, the Board can make such a deduction. (In a divorce case the Board can only make such a deduction on any sum you receive of over £2,500.) It is important therefore in these circumstances to attempt to make a claim for the costs of the action against your opponent.

Q. If I do not qualify for legal aid to raise a court action, what are my options?

A. You are entitled to appeal against the refusal of legal aid. If the appeal is unsuccessful you would either require to pay your lawyer privately or attempt to conduct the case yourself without the assistance of a lawyer. Your local Citizens Advice Bureau or sheriff clerk may give you help in this connection.

Criminal Legal Aid

The criminal legal aid system works extremely well. By and large, anyone who is not particularly well off and has a reasonable defence will be granted legal aid (provided the charge is not too minor).

This was not always the case. In District Court cases the decision as to whether or not the client should receive legal aid used to lie with the Magistrate in question. Most exercised their discretion very sensibly but there were notable exceptions. I recall acting for a 16-year-old client who had no history of criminality. He was charged with throwing a brick through a shop window. We had six witnesses (one of whom was an Elder with the Church of Scotland, no less) who were prepared to confirm that he was nowhere near the shop on the night in question. The Magistrate refused legal aid because he thought the defence was so good that the young lad could defend himself without a lawyer. Nowadays legal aid would almost certainly be granted for such a case.

Q. Can I obtain criminal legal aid even if I have not actually been charged or have received a summons?

A. Yes. You are entitled to legal aid for general advice. This is known as 'advice and assistance' (*see* CIVIL LEGAL AID *for financial details*).

Q. If I am charged with an offence and simply wish to plead Guilty, am I still entitled to legal aid?

A. Yes. You are normally entitled to legal aid to cover representation by your lawyer in court.

Q. What is the legal aid position if I am charged and wish to plead Not Guilty to the charges?

A. You require to apply to the Legal Aid Board for a Legal Aid Certificate. The Board will normally grant you legal aid if you are financially eligible and if you have a reasonable defence to the charges against you.

Q. Do I require to have defence witnesses before the Legal Aid Board will grant me legal aid?

A. No, although reference to such defence witnesses will enhance your chances of obtaining legal aid.

231

Q. If I am unhappy with the services of my lawyer, can I change to another one?

A. The Legal Aid Board will usually agree to a transfer of the Legal Aid Certificate to another lawyer, provided you can show good cause for such a change. A transfer can be made by the Board even if your first lawyer objects to it.

Q. Is there a limit to the amount of work my lawyer can do under the Legal Aid Certificate?

A. Generally, no. Your lawyer is entitled to carry out any work which he considers is reasonably necessary for the full preparation of your defence.

Q. Is there a different procedure for legal aid if I am charged with a very serious offence?

A. If you are charged with a very serious offence you would usually be detained overnight in a police cell and appear in court the next day. On that day, the Procurator Fiscal will produce a document called a Petition, which contains the charges against you. In these circumstances your lawyer should ask the sheriff to grant legal aid at that first court appearance. All you require to prove is that you are financially eligible for legal aid. You do not have to prove that you have a reasonable defence.

Q. Is legal aid available for all criminal offences?

A. Usually the Legal Aid Board is reluctant to grant legal aid if the offence is relatively minor. It would be very difficult to obtain legal aid for certain road traffic offences such as speeding, for example.

Q. Do I have to pay anything to the Legal Aid Board as a contribution towards the cost of my defence (similar to the position with civil legal aid)?

A. No. If you are granted legal aid then no contribution is sought from you.

Q. If I am refused legal aid, what are my options?

A. You are entitled to appeal against the refusal of legal aid. If the appeal is unsuccessful you would either require to pay your solicitor privately or attempt to defend yourself without the assistance of a lawyer.

Appendices

Citizens Advice Bureaux

Please note that, in accordance with British Telecom's imminent changes, all area dialling codes which currently begin '0-' will become '01-' after April 1995.

Borders

25 Albert Place
GALASHIELS
TD1 3DL
Tel. (0896) 3889

15A High Street
HAWICK
TD5 7AL
Tel. (0450) 74266

42 Old Town
PEEBLES
EH45 8JF
Tel. (0721) 721722

Central

47 Drysdale Street
ALLOA
FK10 1JA
Tel. (0259) 723880
Old Sheriff Court
Hope Street
FALKIRK
FK1
Tel. (0324) 28406

The Norman
MacEwan Centre
Cameronian Street
STIRLING
FK8 2DX
**Tel. (0786)
470239/470257**

35 Church Walk
Denny
STIRLING
FK6 6DF
**Tel. (0324)
823118/825333**

Dumfries and Galloway

3 St Andrews Street
CASTLE DOUGLAS
G67 1DE
Tel. (0556) 502190

164 High Street
DUMFRIES
DG1 2BA
Tel. (0387) 52456

14 Hanover Street
STRANRAER
DG9 7RZ
Tel. (0776) 2431

Fife

322 High Street
COWDENBEATH
KY4 9NT
Tel. (0383) 513151

119 Canmore Road
GLENROTHES
KY7 4BJ
Tel. (0592) 753382

10 Union Road
GRANGEMOUTH
FK3 8AB
**Tel. (0324)
486343/483467**

11 Wemyssfield
KIRKCALDY
KY1 1XN
Tel. (0592) 264021

Wellesley Road
METHIL
KY8 3QR
Tel. (0333) 424993

158 South Street
ST ANDREWS
Tel. (0334) 73077

Grampian

47 Market Street
ABERDEEN
AB1 2PZ
Tel. (0224) 586255

Voluntary
Information Centre
Unit 5
Business Centre
ABOYNE
AB3 5HE
Tel. (03398) 87005

4 Bridge Street
BANCHORY
AB31 3SX
Tel. (03302) 5551

Ellon Area Advice
Centre
Inverythan House
The Square
ELLON
AB41 9JB
Tel. (0358) 724425

149 High Street
FORRES
IV36 0DX
Tel. (0309) 675215

76 Frithside Street
FRASERBURGH
AB4 5JA
Tel. (0346) 25307

Gordon Rural Action
& Information
Network
53–55 Gordon Street
HUNTLY
AB54 5EQ
Tel. (0466) 793676

Railway Station
Building
INVERURIE
AB5 9TN
Tel. (0467) 24421

14 Reidhaven Square
KEITH
AB5 3AB
Tel. (05422) 887995

Bervie Advice Service
27 Gladstone Place
LAURENCEKIRK
AB30 1DX
Tel. (0561) 62039

Marischal Chambers
Drummers Corner
PETERHEAD
AB42
Tel. (0779) 71515

Stonehaven Advice
and Information
Resource
2A Market Lane
STONEHAVEN
AB3 2BW
Tel. (0569) 66578

Turriff Resource
Advice and
Information Centre
Masonic Buildings
Gladstone Terrace
TURRIFF
AB53 7UH
Tel. (0888) 62495

Highland

4 Novar Road
ALNESS
IV1 80QG
Tel. (0349) 883333

The Old Library
Dudley Road
FORT WILLIAM
PH33 6BA
Tel. (0397) 705311

103 Academy Street
INVERNESS
IV1 1LX
Tel. (0463) 235345

Grant Street
NAIRN
IV12 4NN
Tel. (0667) 55234

7A Brabster Street
THURSO
KW14 7AP
Tel. (0847) 64243

ISLANDS

Castlebay
BARRA
PA80 5XD
Tel. (0871) 210608

'Highfield'
Bowmore
ISLAY
PA43 7JE
Tel. (049681) 669

Old Hostel
Tarbet
HARRIS
Tel. (0859) 502431

2 Bells Road
Stornoway
LEWIS
PA87 2QT
Tel. (0851) 705727

Anchor Buildings
8 Bridge Street
Kirkwall
ORKNEY
KW15 1HR
Tel. (0856) 875266

45 Commercial
Street
Lerwick
SHETLAND
ZE1 0AN
Tel. (0595) 4696

Skye and Lochalsh
Community and
Advice Centre
Elgin Hostel
Portree
SKYE
IV51 9HA
Tel. (0478) 2032

7 Druim Na H'airde
Balivanich
UIST
PA88 5LS
Tel. (0870) 602421

Lothian

46 Hopetoun Street
BATHGATE
EH48 4EU
Tel. (0506) 634305

8 Buccleuch Street
DALKEITH
EH22 1HA
**Tel. (0131)
663 3688/660 1636**

EDINBURGH

58 Dundas Street
EH3 6QZ
**Tel. (0131)
557 1500**

661 Ferry Road
Pilton
EH4 2TX
**Tel. (0131)
332 9434**

Edinburgh Chinese
Elderly Support
Association
25 Home Street
Tollcross
EH3 9JR
**Tel. (0131)
228 5808**

268 Gorgie Road
EH11 2PP
**Tel. (0131)
337 6353**

166 Great Junction
Street
Leith
EH6 5LJ
**Tel. (0131)
554 8144**

1 Murrayburn Street
Wester Hailes
EH14 2SS
**Tel. (0131)
442 2424**

191 Portobello High
Street
EH15 1EU
**Tel. (0131)
669 7138**

Breich Valley
Information Service
21 Blackfaulds Place
FAULDHOUSE
EH47 9AS
Tel. (0501) 70276

38 Market Street
HADDINGTON
EH41 3JE
**Tel. (062 082)
4471**

Unit 7
Sheil House
Craigshill
LIVINGSTON
EH54 5EH
Tel. (0506) 32977

141 High Street
MUSSELBURGH
EH21 7DD
**Tel. (0131)
653 2748/2544**

14A John Street
PENICUIK
EH26 8AB
Tel. (0698) 675259

Strathclyde

14 Anderson Street
Resource Centre
AIRDRIE
ML6 0AA
**Tel. (0236)
754109/754376**

Park Terrace
Lamlash
ARRAN
KA27 8NB
Tel. (07706) 210

Unemployed Workers
Resource Centre
1 Mainholm Road
AYR
KA8 0QF
Tel. (0292) 286785

216 Main Street
BARRHEAD
G78 1SN
**Tel. (0141)
881 2032**

6 Hamilton Road
BELLSHILL
ML4 1AQ
Tel. (0698) 748615

Blantyre Information
& Money Advice
Calder Street
BLANTYRE
G72 0AU
Tel. (0698) 828383

42 Kilbowie Road
CLYDEBANK
G81 1TH
**Tel. (0141)
952 7921/7923**

31 Lennox Drive
Faifley
CLYDEBANK
G81
Tel. (0389) 890105

240

25 Academy Street
COATBRIDGE
ML5 3AW
**Tel. (0236)
421447/421448**

2 Annan House
Third Floor
CUMBERNAULD
G67 1DP
Tel. (0236) 723201

22 College Way
DUMBARTON
G82 1LJ
**Tel. (0389)
61380/65345**

Cornwall Street
EAST KILBRIDE
G74 1QB
Tel. (03552) 21295

GLASGOW

Hellenic House
Third Floor
87–89 Bath Street
G2 2EE
**Tel. (0141)
331 2345**

119 Main Street
Bridgeton
G40 1QD
**Tel. (0141)
554 0336**

27 Dougrie Drive
Castlemilk
G45
**Tel. (0141)
634 0338/0339**

49 Dunkenny Square
Drumchapel
G15 8NE
**Tel. (0141)
944 2612**

46 Shandwick
Square
Easterhouse
G34 9DS
**Tel. (0141)
771 2328**

One Plus
39 Hope Street
GLASGOW
G2 6AE
**Tel. (0141)
221 7150**

Scottish Asian Action
Committee
4 Labelle Place
GLASGOW
G3 7LH
**Tel. (0141)
331 1069**

1145 Maryhill Road
Maryhill
G20 9AZ
**Tel. (0141)
946 6373/6374**

1361–63 Gallowgate
Parkhead
G31 4DN
**Tel. (0141)
554 0004**

139 Main Street
RUTHERGLEN
G73 2JJ
**Tel. (0141)
647 5100**

Community
Resource and
Information Service
Unit 9
Ravenscraig
Shopping Precinct
Larkfield
GREENOCK
PA16 0UD
Tel. (01475) 637474

67 Almada Street
HAMILTON
ML3 0HQ
Tel. (0698) 283477

65 Titchfield Street
KILMARNOCK
KA1 1QS
Tel. (0563) 44744

Clydesdale Advice
Service
19 Wellgate
LANARK
ML11 7NE
Tel. (0555) 664301

32 Civic Square
MOTHERWELL
ML1 3TP
**Tel. (0698)
251981/259389**

45 George Street
PAISLEY
PA1 2JY
**Tel. (0141)
889 2121**

98 Dockhead Street
SALTCOATS
KA21 5EL
Tel. (0294) 67848

Tayside

92 High Street
ARBROATH
DD11 1HL
Tel. (0241) 70661

97 Seagate
DUNDEE
DD1 2EH
**Tel. (0382)
27171/27172**

106 Castle Street
FORFAR
DD8 3HR
Tel. (0307) 467097

38 Murray Street
MONTROSE
DD10 8LB
Tel. (0674) 73263

6-12 New Row
PERTH
PH1 5QB
Tel. (0738) 24301

Sheriff Courts

Borders

Duns Sheriff Court
Castlegate
JEDBURGH
TD8 6AP
DX Box No 1222
Tel. (0361) 83719

Jedburgh Sheriff
Court
Castlegate
JEDBURGH
TD8 6AP
DX Box No 1222
Tel. (0835) 863231

Peebles Sheriff
Court
High Street
PEEBLES
EH45 8SW
DX Box No 971
Tel. (0721) 720204

Selkirk Sheriff Court
Ettrick Terrace
SELKIRK
TD7 4LE
DX Box No 1011
Tel. (0750) 21269

Central

Alloa Sheriff Court
County Buildings
Mar Street
ALLOA
FK10 1HR
DX Box No 433
Tel. (0259) 722734

Falkirk Sheriff Court
Main Street
Camelon
FALKIRK
FK1 4AR
DX Box No FA17
Tel. (0324) 620822

Kirkcaldy Sheriff
Court
Whytecauseway
KIRKCALDY
KY1 1XQ
DX Box No KY17
Tel. (0592) 260171

Stirling Sheriff Court
Viewfield Place
STIRLING
FK8 1NH
DX Box No ST15
Tel. (0786) 462191

Dumfries and Galloway

Dumfries Sheriff Court
Buccleuch Street
DUMFRIES
DG1 2AN
DX Box No 617
Tel. (0387) 62334

Kirkcudbright
Sheriff Court
High Street
KIRKCUDBRIGHT
DG6 4JP
DX Box No 812
Tel. (0557) 330574

Fife

Cupar Sheriff Court
County Building
St Catherine's Street
CUPAR
KY15 4LX
DX Box No 545
Tel. (0334) 52121

Dunfermline Sheriff
Court
1-6 Carnegie Drive
DUNFERMLINE
KY12 7HJ
DX Box No DF17
Tel. (0383) 724666

Grampian

Aberdeen Sheriff
Court
Castle Street
ABERDEEN
AB9 1AP
DX Box No AB61
Tel. (0224) 648316

Banff Sheriff Court
Low Street
BANFF
AB4 1AU
DX Box No 1325
Tel. (0261) 812140

Elgin Sheriff Court
High Street
ELGIN
IV30 1BU
DX Box No 652
Tel. (0343) 542505

Peterhead Sheriff
Court
Queen Street
PETERHEAD
AB4 6TP
DX Box No 1376
Tel. (0779) 76676

Stonehaven Sheriff
Court
Dunnottar Avenue
STONEHAVEN
AB3 2JH
DX Box No 1023
Tel. (0569) 762758

Highland

Dingwall Sheriff
Court
Ferry Road
DINGWALL
IV15 9QX
DX Box No 584
Tel. (0349) 63153

Dornoch Sheriff Court
Castle Street
DORNOCH
IV25 3FD
Tel. (0862) 310224

Fort William Sheriff
Court
High Street
FORT WILLIAM
PH33 6EE
DX Box No 1405
Tel. (0397) 702087

Inverness Sheriff
Court
The Castle
INVERNESS
IV2 3EG
DX Box No IN25
Tel. (0463) 230782

Tain Sheriff Court
High Street
TAIN
IV19 1AB
Tel. (0862) 892518

Wick Sheriff Court
Bridge Street
WICK
KW1 4AJ
Tel. (0955) 2846

ISLANDS

Stornoway Sheriff
Court
Lewis Street
Stornoway
LEWIS
PA87 2JF
Tel. (0851) 702231

Lochmaddy Sheriff
Court
NORTH UIST
PA82 5AE
Tel. (0876) 500340

Kirkwall Sheriff
Court
Watergate
Kirkwall
ORKNEY
KW15 1PD
Tel. (0856) 872110

Lerwick Sheriff
Court
King Erik Street
Lerwick
SHETLAND
Tel. (0595) 3914

Portree Sheriff Court
Somerled Square
Portree
SKYE
IV51 9EH
Tel. (0478) 612191

Lothian

Edinburgh Sheriff
Court
37 Chambers Street
EDINBURGH
EH1 1LB
DX Box No ED308
**Tel. (0131)
225 2525**

Haddington Sheriff
Court
Court Street
HADDINGTON
EH41 3HN
DX Box No 732
Tel. (062082) 2936

Linlithgow Sheriff
Court
High Street
LINLITHGOW
EH49 7EQ
DX Box No 881
Tel. (0506) 842922

Strathclyde

Airdrie Sheriff Court
Graham Street
AIRDRIE
ML6 6EE
DX Box No 416
Tel. (0236) 751121

Ayr Sheriff Court
Wellington Square
AYR
KA7 1DR
DX Box No AY16
Tel. (0292) 268474

Campbeltown
Sheriff Court
Main Street
CAMPBELTOWN
PA28 9QJ
Tel. (0586) 552503

Dumbarton Sheriff
Court
Church Street
DUMBARTON
G82 1QR
DX Box No 597
Tel. (0389) 763266

Dunoon Sheriff
Court
George Street
DUNOON
PA23 8BQ
Tel. (0369) 4166

Glasgow Sheriff
Court
1 Carlton Place
GLASGOW
DX Box No GW213
**Tel. (0141)
429 8888**

Greenock Sheriff
Court
Nelson Street
GREENOCK
DX Box No GR16
Tel. (0475) 787673

Hamilton Sheriff
Court
Almada Street
HAMILTON
ML3 0HR
DX Box No HA16
Tel. (0698) 282957

Kilmarnock Sheriff
Court
St Marnock Street
KILMARNOCK
KA1 1ED
DX Box No KK20
Tel. (0563) 20211

Lanark Sheriff
Court
Hope Street
LANARK
ML11 7NQ
DX Box No 832
Tel. (0555) 661531

Oban Sheriff Court
Albany Street
OBAN
PA34 4AL
DX Box No OB8
Tel. (0631) 62414

Paisley Sheriff
Court
St James Street
PAISLEY
PA3 2HW
DX Box No PA48
**Tel. (0141)
887 5291**

Rothesay Sheriff
Court
Castle Street
ROTHESAY
PA20 9HA
Tel. (0700) 50 2982

Stranraer Sheriff
Court
Lewis Street
STRANRAER
DG9 7AA
DX Box No 1261
Tel. (0776) 702138

Tayside

Arbroath Sheriff Court
Town House
88 High Street
ARBROATH
DD11 1HL
DX Box No 442
Tel. (0241) 876600

Dundee Sheriff Court
6 West Bell Street
DUNDEE
DD1 9DA
DX Box No DD33
**Tel. (0382)
29961 or 26513**

Forfar Sheriff Court
Market Street
FORFAR
DD8 3LA
DX Box No 674
Tel. (0307) 462186

Perth Sheriff Court
Tay Street
PERTH
PH2 8NL
DX Box No PE20
Tel. (0738) 20546

Helplines

EMPLOYMENT
SERVICES
Argyle House
3 Lady Lawson Street
Edinburgh
EH3 9DR
0131 229 9191

**Equal
Opportunities
Commission**
St Andrew House
141 West Nile Street
Glasgow
G1 2RN
0141 332 8018

INDUSTRIAL
RELATIONS
ACAS (Advisory
Conciliation &
Arbitration)
Grayfield House

Bankhead Avenue
Edinburgh
EH11 4AA
0131 453 2525

ACAS
Franborough House
123-57 Bothwell
Street
Glasgow
G2 7BR
0141 204 2677

INLAND REVENUE
Tax Enquiry Centre
Stuart House
30 Semple Street
Edinburgh
EH3 8JX
0131 228 6661

**Tax Enquiry
Centre**
Hamilton House
20 Waterloo Street
Glasgow
G2 6DB
0141 204 0071

VEHICLE
REGISTRATION
OFFICES
**Department of
Transport**
Saughton House
Broomhouse Drive
Edinburgh
EH1 3XE
0131 455 7919

**Department of
Transport**
107 Bothwell Street
Glasgow
G2 7EE
0141 226 4161

DVLC
Swansea
SA99 1AR
0792 782341

HEALTH AUTHORITIES
**Lothian Health
Board**
The Pleasance
Edinburgh
EH8 9RR
0131 229 5888

**Greater Glasgow
Health Board**
112 Ingram Street
Glasgow
G1 1ET
0141 552 6222

COMMUNITY
RELATIONS
**Lothian Racial
Equality Council**
12A Forth Street
Edinburgh
EH1 3LH
0131 556 0441

**Strathclyde
Community
Relations Council**
115 Wellington
Street
Glasgow
G2 2XT
0141 227 6048

POLICE
**Crimestoppers
0800 555111**
*If you have informa-
tion regarding a crime,
ring this number. You
can remain anony-
mous and you may
receive a Community
Action Trust Award.*

DATA PROTECTION
**Data Protection
Registrar**
Wycliffe House
Water Lane
Wilmslow
SK9 5AF
0625 535777
*Handles complaints
against computer
users, concerning out-
of-date or inaccurate
personal information.*

DEBT
National Debtline
318 Summer Lane
Birmingham
B19 3LR
0121 359 8501
*24-hour answerphone.
Free confidential
advice on mortgages,
rent arrears and other
debts.*

HOUSING ADVICE
**Edinburgh District
Council**
27 Waterloo Place
Edinburgh
EH1 3BH
**0131 225 2424
ext 7368**

**Glasgow City
Council Housing
Service**
Lomond House
9 George Square
Glasgow
G2 1TG
0141 221 9600

LEGAL SERVICES
**Solicitors'
Complaints Bureau
071 834 8663**

TRADING STANDARDS
Advice Shop
85/87 South Bridge
Edinburgh
EH1 1HN
0131 225 1255

Advice Shop
1 St Enoch Square
Glasgow
G1 4BH
0141 204 0262

CRIME VICTIMS
Lothian Victim Support Scheme
15 Calton Hill
Edinburgh
EH1 3BJ
0131 556 1718

Strathclyde Victim Support
10 Jocelyn Square
Glasgow
G1
0141 553 1726

Parents of Murdered Children Group
92 Corbets Tey Road
Upminster
RM14 2BA
0708 640400

DIVORCED AND SEPARATED
Families Need Fathers
BM–Families
London
WC1N 3XX
0181 886 0970
Offers help for non-custodial parents and their children.

Lothian Family Mediation Service
37 George Street
Edinburgh
EH2 2HN
0131 226 4507
A service to help separating and divorcing couples to settle disputes, especially over children.

FAMILY AND CHILDREN
Childline
Call free of charge
0800 1111
For children in trouble or danger.

Exploring Parenthood Helpline
0181 960 1678
Support, advice and counselling for all parents dealing with problems or difficulties in the family.

Family Rights Group
The Print House
18 Ashwin Street
London
E8 3DL
0171 249 0008
Help for families with children in care or undergoing child protection procedures

National Stepfamily Association
72 Willesden Lane
London
NW6 7TA
0171 372 0846

RSSPCC
Melville House
41 Polwarth Terrace
Edinburgh
EH11 1NU
0131 337 8539

RSSPCC
Annfield Family Resource Centre
15 Annfield Place
Dennistoun
Glasgow
G31 1XE
0141 556 1156

HOMELESS
Shelter Housing Aid Centre
103 Morrison Street
Edinburgh
EH3 8BX
0131 229 8771

Shelter Housing Aid Centre
53 St Vincent Crescent
Glasgow
G3
0141 221 8995

MARRIAGE GUIDANCE
**Marriage
Counselling
Service**
9A Dundas Street
Edinburgh
EH3 6QG
0131 556 1527
*Open Mon to Thur
9 a.m.–9 p.m., Fri
9 a.m.–2 p.m. and Sat
10 a.m.–1 p.m.*

**Marriage
Counselling
Service**
27 Sandyford Place
Glasgow
G3
0141 248 5249

ONE-PARENT FAMILIES
Gingerbread
19 Chester Street
Edinburgh
EH3 7RF
0131 220 1585

Gingerbread
Strathclyde
Federation
304 Maryhill Road
Glasgow G20
0141 353 0989

**Scottish Council
for Single Parents**
13 Gayfield Square
Edinburgh
EH1 3NX
0131 556 3899

**Scottish Council
for Single Parents**
One Plus
One-Parent Families
Strathclyde
39 Hope Street
Glasgow
G2
0141 248 3488

RAPE
**Edinburgh Rape
Crisis Centre**
PO Box 120
Edinburgh
EH1 3RJ
0131 556 9437
24-hour answerphone.

Rape Crisis Centre
(Strathclyde)
PO Box 53
Glasgow
G2
0141 221 8448

Samaritans
54 Frederick Street
Edinburgh
EH1 2LN
0131 225 3333
*24-hour emergency
service for the suicidal
and despairing.*

Samaritans
210 West George
Street
Glasgow
G2
0141 248 4488

WOMEN'S AID
**Edinburgh
Women's Aid**
97/101 Morrison Street
Edinburgh
EH3 8BX
0131 229 1419

Women's Aid
(Glasgow)
30 Bell Street
Glasgow
G1 1LG
0141 553 2022

**Scottish Women's
Aid**
13 North Bank Street
Edinburgh
EH1 2LP
**0131
225 8011/3321**
*Temporary accommoda-
tion for physically, men-
tally or sexually abused
women and their chil-
dren.*

Glossary

aliment – maintenance payable to children (or to a spouse prior to decree of divorce)

alimony – the English equivalent of aliment

capital sum – payment sought by one spouse against the other upon divorce

co-habitation – spouses or partners living together

court order or **decree –** an award or decision made by a court

courts

    Court of Session – the highest civil court in Scotland where important civil cases are heard

    High Court – the highest criminal court in Scotland where very serious crimes are dealt with

    District Court – where less serious crimes are dealt with

    Sheriff Court – where most other civil and criminal cases are dealt with

curator – someone appointed by the court to manage another's affairs

defamation – the malicious communication of a false statement or idea which defames or insults you

estate – property owned by someone at time of death

interim assessment – calculation made by the Child Support Agency of the liability of someone to pay aliment who has not co-operated with the Agency in divulging his/her financial position

interim exclusion order - court order forbidding a spouse or partner from living in the family home

interim interdict - court order granted during the course of a court action forbidding someone from doing something until a final decision is made in that court action

maintenance - money paid by one spouse to another to maintain that spouse or by one partner or spouse to another to maintain the children of that spouse or partner

periodical allowance - maintenance paid by one spouse to another upon or after decree of divorce

on petition - criminal court system when you are charged with a serious offence or offences

poinding - necessary procedure to be carried out by Sheriff Officers prior to a warrant sale (*see below*)

right of access - the right to have contact with your children

sheriff officer - an officer with the right to, for instance, serve writs and enforce decrees by arranging poindings and warrant sales

spouse - husband or wife

summons - writ which is lodged in court

to reduce a will - to have the court set aside a will so it has no legal effect

warrant sale - procedure carried out by Sheriff Officers by which your goods are sold to pay off your debt or debts